Berkeley Mediation
and Well Being Institute
PO Box 7222
Berkeley, California 94707
Phone: (510) 867-9616
Google Voice: (011)(510) 984-4581
Skype: pepper.black
Email: pepperblackinberkeley@gmail.com
Website: www.

I Got'Cho Back!

Improving Relationships with Young Black Males

By

Aaron Horn

I GOT'CHO BACK!

To my auntie Paulette, thank you for teaching me about making money and for hustling. Your teaching inspired me to have a job ever since I was in high school. I am so thankful for your mentoring at such a young age.

To my auntie Lisa, thank you for babysitting me when mom needed some help. You always were there to help raise me and you have been a phenomenal auntie. Thank you for being the organizer of the family and for keeping the family organized since grandma's passing.

In addition, I am praying for you every day as you are battling with and will eventually win your fight with breast cancer. I will continue to visit with you every day until we have won this fight! I love you!

To Uncle Craig, thank you for teaching me how to maintain my sanity in a world that is often challenging to me as a Black man. I am proud to have you as my Uncle. You and Auntie Lisa represent the soul of the distinguished Black couple!

Also, thank you for taking care of my aunt as she fights this pernicious disease. God chose the right partner for my auntie when he brought you two together. I am so thankful that you are in her life to help her win this fight! I love you very much!

To my Auntie Robey and Uncle Eddie, thank you for helping my mom raise me as a child, especially for chastising me when I was "off da hook" as we say in the Black community! Your reprimand allowed me to grow up respecting my elders – taking heed to your advice!

ACKNOWLEDGMENTS

As always, I give the highest thanks and praise to God! Thank you for giving me the gift of caregiving for children. To my African ancestors, thank you for offering your souls in exchange for the new generation of Black leaders who are emerging.

To my immediate family (Mom, Marc, and Rita) thank you for supporting my dreams and effort. To granddad, thank you for always pushing me to achieve all of my goals, regardless of what anyone tells me.

To mom (Ursulanda Horn), thank you for raising me into an intelligent, observant, critically conscious human being. Most of all, thank you for never backing down when Marc and I challenged you growing up. I will never forget your fearlessness as a single mother.

Mom, your daily prayers, unconditional love, and unyielding encouragement caused me to become a strong Black male committed to providing effective caregiving skills (counseling, mentoring, and teaching) to other Black males - you cultivated the leader within me!

To grandma, although you passed away two years ago I can feel your spirit resonate within me. I miss you fondly and look forward to joining you in heaven one day.

To the Reynolds, Moore, Parish, Threadgill, Gillette, Jackson and other families, thank you for never giving up on me.

To all of my aunts, uncles, and cousins (Jan, Paulette, Danny, Lisa, Craig, Jeannie, Lucias, Demetrius, Donnell, Janetta, Chris Moore, and Chris Horn). Thank you for supporting my dreams!

To my auntie Jan, thank you for always being there for me. I will never forget your perpetual love. I will always love you and respect you for the moments in my life where you "stepped up" and called me out on my stuff!

TABLE OF CONTENTS

FOREWORD

As Associate Professor and Program Coordinator of the Marriage and Family Therapy program in the Counseling Psychology Department at the University of San Francisco, I feel honored to have been given a forum to express my gratitude to Dr. Aaron Lamont Horn and his continuous passion for dedicating his time and writing about the experiences of young Black males. Not only does Dr. Horn's writing eloquently describe the meaning and purpose of creating and fostering genuine caring relationships with young Black males, but he also shares those emotional experiences from his practice that have continually shaped his life's work as an educator, consultant, and most recently, as a therapist.

I first met Dr. Horn immediately following his doctoral studies in International and Multicultural Education at USF, when he initially contemplated about becoming a therapist. What struck me most about Dr. Horn was not just his warm smile and engaging personality, but rather, a clear, directed and prominent vision of how he could actually effect change in his community; a community in great need and one that is wrought with trauma, pain, fear, and loss. During our meeting, Dr. Horn discussed his desire to work with young Black males and outlined a specific plan to help them thrive and succeed. When he left my office that day, it was completely evident to me that in the future Dr. Aaron Horn was going to do something very important for other people.

Just as we saw in his first book, "The Role of Father-Like Care in the Education of Young Black Males," Dr. Horn continues to defend the importance of caring relationships with young Black males as they mature over their lifespan development. Most significantly, we see his experiences come to life and learn about how Dr. Horn skillfully utilizes his self-developed hybrid counseling technique, consisting of narrative and experiential family therapy, to counsel and support a young adolescent client named DJ through a difficult life transition.

Dr. Horn's manuscript significantly contributes to the scholarly research field on Black males because of the comprehensive research he used as a framework to support his rationale for authentic relationships, particularly their significance to young Black males who are excessively suspended in school, incarcerated in the juvenile justice system, and exposed to trauma. Dr. Horn clearly and passionately supports his justification for caring relationships throughout his research and even begins his prose with the statement, "I am interested in improving relationships." Drawing from the tenets of Bowlby, Ainsworth, and Rogers, Dr. Horn highlights the prominent roles positive attachment and the development of strong relationships play within all contexts of psychological and emotional growth throughout the lifespan.

Most striking are the multiple analyses that Dr. Horn provides regarding the factors that cause young Black males to fail within their perspective communities - namely institutionalized racism. This consistent contextualization considerably enhances the scholarship of his manuscript and gives the reader a greater understanding of the legacy of trauma for Black males. Furthermore, Dr. Horn provides thorough research on specific teaching and therapeutic modalities that have shown to be effective with young Black males in every chapter as a means to support his argument. For example, in Chapter 9 of "I Got'Cho Back," we find Dr. Horn's description of his successful use of cognitive behavioral therapy to help Black males of color recapitulate their negative schema (i.e., negative thinking) into a more positively focused mind-set. In essence, Dr. Horn provides a step-by-step, easy-to-follow process of how educators, therapists, and lay people can use his powerfully inspirational tool, the Horn Accountability Instrument (H.A.I.), to transform the minds of young Black males all across America.

Finally, after reading and reflecting on his comprehensive contextualizations, excerpts from participants, and personal insights, we understand why Dr. Horn is so passionate about creating and maintaining authentic relationships with young Black males. In fact, his emphasis on accountability to others reflects an acute understanding of what it really takes to build these authentic relationships. This is especially true when we consider that survival, actually staying alive, is often dependent upon a self-focused and cautious interpersonal stance. While this coping behavior may work in the short run, it hinders positive growth and development over the lifespan, as well as the ability to truly connect with others. Most noteworthy, all of Dr. Horn's analyses are enclosed within multiple citations of diverse scholarly references, highlighting the manuscript's evidence-based credibility. As a result, Dr. Horn's critical investigation with young Black males, concerning both the importance of establishing and maintaining caring relationships as well as developing feelings of accountability towards others, is quite ground-breaking and makes us wonder why we didn't think of this before.

Dr. Cori Bussolari

University of San Francisco

Dr. Cori Bussolari is an Associate Professor in the Department of Counseling Psychology at the University of San Francisco. She is also the current Program Coordinator of the Marriage and Family Therapy Program and is a licensed psychologist in private practice in San Francisco, CA.

PREFACE

I am interested in improving relationships (i.e., caring relationships) between all of those who work with high-risk, young Black males because of the disproportionate amount of adolescent Black males who live in poverty, succumb to violence in their community, endure inadequate education, and experience high rates of juvenile incarceration (Horn, 2010; Kunjufu, 2005; Losen & Orfield, 2002; McGoldrick, Giordano, & Garcia-Preto, 2005; National Center for Health Statistics, 2010; Noguera, 2008).

Therefore, I have researched the broader issues that have a significant impact on Black males' lifespan development in order to improve relationships with professionals and lay people who provide caregiving for young Black males. Some of these issues that impact the lifespan development of Black males include: (1) identity development, (2) inadequate education, (3) Black English Vernacular, and (4) indulgent parenting. As a means to provide tools for those who work with high-risk, young Black males, I provide information regarding effective parenting and therapeutic methods that have shown positive results in my work with high-risk, young Black males. To preserve confidentiality, all clients described in this book have pseudonyms.

What Does It Mean to Relate?

It is important for all of us who work in the human service field to understand the concepts of caring relationships and know how to establish them. But, in order to care authentically for someone, I believe you have to be skilled in relating with others, namely, understanding the procedure and impact of human beings' ability to relate (i.e., relatedness) including the importance of language, attachment, attentive care-giving, physical presence, limbic regulation, and neurotransmitters. I believe that all of these aspects collectively impact our ability to relate as a human being.

Lewis et al. (2000) describe that language plays a significant role in a human's ability to relate with others. The authors mention that loss of language has killed many infants in previous studies. For instance, the authors disclose that Frederick II, King of Southern Italy, forbid foster-mothers to speak with young infants while he observed the effects of language elimination on their development. As a result, the infants eventually died.

Attachment can affect a human's ability to relate to others because of the development of proximity that occurs between a mother and her child. Lewis et al. (2000) identify how John Bowlby's studies on mother-child relationship interactions shed light on the importance of attachment in a child's development. Bowlby revealed that when an infant is seeking a desired need, the infant's brain is wired to address those needs. For example, if an infant is hungry, frightened, or uncomfortable, the infant will cry to gain attention. Upon hearing the infant's crying, a mother or caregiver will attend to those needs. Bowlby claimed that infants are wired to emit sounds as a form of proximity survival. I will discuss the concepts of Bowlby's attachment theory in detail in the chapters to follow.

Similarly, Lewis et al. (2000) explain how psychologist Mary Ainsworth took Bowlby's study to another level of attachment – attentive care-giving skills. Ainsworth suggested that mother-child relationships depended on the attentiveness of the mother to her child's needs. In other words, when a child desires for a certain need to be met, the mother responds with a specific, deliberate reaction. For example, if an infant reached out for a hug, the mother would hug the infant, but would release the infant when she felt the infant wanted to be let go. Consequently, the mother does not excessively coddle or attend to the infant's needs. Ainsworth reported that this type of parenting would produce a secure child – one "…who used his mother as a safe haven from which to explore the world" (p. 74).

Relatedness also involves physical presence. Lewis et al. (2000) describe low heart rate and lack of sleep in humans as physiological reactions that are caused by isolation - a loss of physical presence from others. The authors also divulge the results of another study of baby rats having low heart rates when their mother is absent. The authors explain the impact on these baby rats as "…an infant loses all his organizing channels at once…his physiology collapses into the huddled heap of despair…" (p. 83). For this reason, the loss of physical presence can be similarly detrimental to a human's ability to exist as it is in the case of mammals.

Neurotransmitters are key factors in human beings' ability to relate. Lewis et al. (2000) disclose that we have three essential neurotransmitters: serotonin, opiates, and oxytocin. The authors report that physicians have used replicas of these chemicals in drugs to help clients balance themselves when they become depressed. Lewis et al. illustrate an account of a client who was severely depressed and trapped in an unhappy relationship for years until the drug serotonin was introduced to the client. They state that "…when she took a serotonin agent, the balance of her sorrows shifted slightly. Loss hurt a little less. She did then what she had been unable to do: leave her lover without intolerable suffering" (p. 93). The lack of these neurotransmitters can cause severe depression in human beings; thus, affecting our ability to relate to others.

Therefore, Lewis et al. (2000) propose that human beings' ability to relate (i.e., relatedness) is necessary for the lifespan development of human beings. Without a sense of being able to relate to others, children can die and people can become physically and emotionally ill. Without the cumulative completion of relatedness techniques that include language, attachment, attentive care-giving, physical presence, and neurotransmitters, human beings cannot experience relatedness. As the authors compellingly express, "…the physiology of relatedness now tell us that attachment penetrates to the neural core of what it means to be a human being…" (p. 76). I believe this to be the overall effect of relatedness. When we learn how to relate to others, we can reach the spirit of other human beings. This spiritual interconnectedness will allow individuals to reach their fullest potential as human beings.

Therefore, it is my hope that this research on issues that impact Black males' lifespan development will motivate those who work with high-risk, young Black males to become more willing to relate (i.e., form caring relationships) with them. Additionally, I anticipate this book to be used in future trainings for teachers, therapists, parents, doctors, attorneys, and lay people to improve their relationships with young Black males. Hence, the title I Got'Cho Back! I would like for young Black males to know and trust that there are others in the world, aside from the Black community, who will support them during their failures and successes.

CHAPTER 1
THE FLUID DEVELOPMENT OF IDENTITY

In order to understand the lifespan development process of some Black males, it is important to expound upon the research regarding how identity development plays a significant role in the lifespan development process. Thus, in this chapter, I will: (1) discuss the fundamental concepts of identity, (2) reflect on identity development across the lifespan, (3) provide a cultural response to identity, and (4) summarize my response. Although research reveals that identity involves static components, I propose that identity development is a fluid process that transpires in different ways among various cultures and individuals.

The Fundamental Concepts of Identity

The American Psychological Association Dictionary of Psychology (2007) defines identity as,

> an individual's sense of self defined by (a) a set of physical and psychological characteristics that is not wholly shared with any other person and (b) a range of social and interpersonal affiliations (e.g. ethnicity) and social roles. Identity involves a sense of continuity: the feeling that one is the same person today that one was yesterday or last year (despite physical or other changes). (p. 463)

On the other hand, Santrock (2009) describes that the concept of identity is formed with three initial features: the materialization of attachment, the development of a sense of self, and the emergence of independence in infancy. Santrock also affirms identity as a self-portrait composed of many components such as career and work, politics, religion, relationship, intelligence, sexuality, culture, interests, personality, and physicality. Santrock further elucidates that identity development occurs "…in bits and pieces…Decisions are not made once and for all, but have to be made again and again…." (p. 385). These foundational definitions reveal that identity is composed of many elements that can be altered during the lifespan, making it a fluid process.

Identity also involves the process of attachment in reciprocal loving relationships, especially with a partner, significant other, or spouse. As described in Santrock (2009), attachment is a key feature of identity development. Parallel to Santrock's views on attachment and identity, Lewis, Amini, and Lannon (2000) discuss attachment with regards to what they name "limbic relationships" in the following passage,

> When somebody loses his partner and says a part of him is gone, he is more right than he thinks. A portion of his neural activity depends on the presence of that other living brain. Without it, the electric interplay that makes up *him* has changed. Lovers hold the keys to each other's identities, and they write neurostructural alterations into each other's networks. Their limbic tie allows each to influence who the other is and becomes. (p. 208)

This powerfully written passage by Lewis et al. (2000) explains that a part of our identity development is due mostly to our attachment to others within mutual loving relationships.

Additional research supports Lewis et al.'s (2000) and Santrock's (2009) belief of why attachment is a key element in identity development. Some of the original attachment theorists posited that attachment involves a unique relationship between a child and its mother (Ainsworth, 1967; Ainsworth & Witing, 1969; Ainsworth, Blehar, Walters, & Wall, 1978; Bowlby, 1969). Although these attachment theorists agreed in the general formation of child-mother attachment, they differed in how it originates.

To clarify the various analyses on being attached, Bowlby (1969) states,

To say of a child that he is attached to, or has an attachment to, someone means that he is strongly disposed to seek proximity to and contact with a specific figure and to do so in certain situations, notably when he is frightened, tired and ill. The disposition to behave in this way is an attribute of the child, an attribute which changes slowly over time and which is unaffected by the situation of the moment... (p. 371)

Bowlby's definition gives us a clear picture of how attachment in mother-child relationships helps support identity development through closeness. Accordingly, individuals develop their identity by being near others - not in isolation.

In particular, Bowlby (1969) pronounces that a child develops an attachment with his caregiver until they reach adolescence. During teenage years, children detach from their primary caregivers and form other healthy or secure attachments with other adults, organizations, and peers. The problem arises when children have an unexpected or lengthened separation from their parent or biological caregiver as a child. This abrupt separation can lead to an unhealthy attachment and other potential psychopathologies in interpersonal relationships as adults, including separation anxiety.

This type of separation anxiety can be seen in one of my clients named Jacob. Jacob is a 12-year-old African American male who lives in an underserved community in San Francisco. During his childhood, Jacob endured abandonment from his father when he was a baby, excessive exposure to community violence, and inadequate education – namely institutionalized racism at his elementary and middle schools. During his middle school years, he began to act out his suppressed emotions by leaving school without permission, being defiant towards adults, and staying out all night with his peers.

As I began to talk with Jacob one-on-one, he disclosed that he was angry that his mom had taken a new job. He was angry that he did not have her available to talk with, prior to his mother acquiring her new job. Thus, in order to release his frustrations, he stayed out all night as a means to cope with his anger and hurt over his perceived abandonment by his mother, which compounded his anger and hurt over the real abandonment of his father. As a result, his newfound friendships with the peers whom he hangs out with at night can be a consequence of his separation anxiety with his mother – resulting in his establishment of unhealthy attachments.

Additionally, Bowlby's (1969) analysis sheds light on the fact that identity development can become distorted throughout the lifespan with individuals who experience unexpected separations as children. In the following section, I will discuss research that explains the various fluid processes and methods that encompass identity development over the lifespan.

Identity Development across the Lifespan

Santrock (2009) explains that identity development changes over the course of a lifespan, beginning in adolescence with more changes taking place in adulthood. During infancy (18 to 24 months), Santrock observes that children are highly dependent on parents. This attachment to parents, as defined earlier, is crucial for language development and social learning. In regards to infant self-awareness, Santrock reports that studies have shown infants to be aware of themselves when rubbing a mirror excessively after viewing their image in the mirror.

This information supports the understanding that identity development, as it relates to awareness, initiates in infancy. During early childhood (5 to 6 years of age), children become independent and prepare for school (Santrock, 2009). In middle and late childhood (6 to 11 years of age), Santrock observes that children become skilled at reading and arithmetic skills. They become aware of achievement and start to realize that their world exists within a larger framework that includes culture. These forms of identity development set the stage for individuals to define themselves early in their lifespan.

Most significant is the research from Santrock (2009) that demonstrates the bulk of identity development occurring in adolescence. In adolescence (10 to 12 through 18 to 21 years of age), identity development consists of physical growth and sexual awareness. Santrock (2009) notes that identity development in adolescence converges to a point where an individual is able to consciously reflect upon the psychosocial, physical, and emotive development that are essential to identity. Regardless, in adolescence, identity development involves experimentation. For instance, Erik Erikson's theory gives us a view of how identity is experimented with and explored during adolescence. In his fifth developmental stage, otherwise known as adolescence, Erikson defines his notion of identity versus identity confusion. For further information on Developmental Stages of Children, see Erikson and Erikson (1998).

In this stage, Santrock (2009) describes Erikson's ideas of this phenomenon as "…adolescents are faced with deciding who they are, what they are all about, and where they are going in life…" (p. 386). By this means, identity development during the course of the adolescent lifespan is inundated with experimentation. Santrock illuminates Erikson's theory by defining that in this fifth stage of adolescent development most adolescents are continuously searching to play diverse roles and experiment with different personalities. For example, recurrent decisions over career explorations such as wanting to be a doctor or a lawyer one minute and then wanting to be a teacher or social worker in the very next minute continuously overwhelms the mind of adolescents.

Similarly, my client Peter (a 15-year-old African American male) can be described to be in Erikson's fifth stage of adolescent development. Throughout the course of 2012, I asked Peter about his aspirations after high school. During a recent session, he mumbled "I dunno…Maybe work a lil' bit….maybe got to City College (a local junior college in San Francisco)…I dunno…" (Peter, Researcher Journal, October 18, 2012). In essence, Peter's scattered thoughts can be attributed to the normalization of experimenting inherent in Erikson's fifth stage of adolescent development.

More to the point, adolescents who successfully resolve their conflicts with identity emerge with a new sense of self-awareness; whereas adolescents who do not resolve these conflicts suffer from identity confusion. These feelings of confusion, as described by Erikson in Santrock (2009), usually cause individuals to take one of two routes: either adolescents isolate themselves from their peers or they immerse themselves amongst peers and lose their identity in the crowd. Therefore, the primary search to understand childhood identity and how it relates to future adult identity development focuses on experimentation during the adolescent phase of the lifespan.

Erikson's points of conflict and resolution can have different meanings for many high-risk, young African American males. For example, my incarcerated client Mickey (a 15-year-old African American male) whom I counseled during a short term in juvenile hall was in full-blown resolution phase of his identity development. Unfortunately, his resolve of being a violent gang member was the identity he had chosen. Mickey had been incarcerated in the Juvenile Justice Center over the years for various violent crimes. Most recently, he was being detained for concealment of a firearm. When I met Mickey in 2011, he discussed in our counseling session his history of violence in some of San Francisco's urban neighborhoods.

Speaking candidly about a particular shooting, Mickey disclosed, "…All I know is the streets…you feel me... I was raised in the streets…when I get out of here…Imma be in them streets…" (Mickey, Researcher Journal, October, 2011). Mickey's steadfast belief of being in and of the streets is normal identity development for many high-risk, young Black males. This identity development allows many Black males to navigate the tumultuous terrain of their underserved communities while earning respect from their peers who also claim the streets in which they live. For more clients' disclosures regarding their adolescent identity development, see Horn (2010).

To expand on Erikson's theory of adolescent identity development, Santrock (2009) describes researcher James Marcia's theory regarding *four statuses of identity* or ways of resolving identity crisis (i.e., identity diffusion, identity foreclosure, identity moratorium, and identity achievement). These four statuses help adolescents decide on their identity as it pertains to the existence or extent of their crisis or commitment. Santrock explains that a crisis involves the phase of identity growth during which the adolescent is exploring options. Commitment is the part of identity progress in which adolescents show personal interest in identity.

As stated by Santrock (2009), Marcia describes that adolescents become categorized into one of the four statuses of identity, depending upon the extent of their crisis and ability to commit to an identity. For example, in Marcia's Four Statuses of Identity, an adolescent identified in the category of Identity Diffusion has neither committed to an identity nor experienced a crisis in adolescence. On the contrary, an adolescent categorized in Identity Achievement has both endured a crisis and is fully committed to an identity. Marcia's notions of identity development spell out that identity is fluid because it articulates the changeability of identity development in adolescence.

Similar to Marcia's Identity Achievement status of identity, many of my young Black male clients develop "street identity" or "street cred" as a form of identity achievement. For example, growing up in extreme poverty, being exposed to violence, and often being involved in violent crimes allows them to develop a street persona. Eventually, this street persona garners respect among their Black peers who are also from the same neighborhood. Whether earned the hard way or through simple endurance, having a street persona validates their right to maintain what Dance (2009) calls a "tough front" – a type of street posturing that earns them automatic respect on the streets.

Sexual identity is an additional factor that adds to the variability of identity development in adolescence. Santrock (2009) recognizes that sexual identity is a complicated and lengthy process. It involves learning to negotiate sexual feelings, developing new forms of intimacy, and regulating sexual behavior to avoid uninvited consequences. In addition, Santrock makes it clear that an adolescent's sexual individuality involves activities, interests, styles of behavior, and an indication of sexual orientation.

Hence, individual sexuality can vary in the lifespan, especially in adolescence. For example, Santrock (2009) observes that some adolescents can have a very high level of sexual activity whereas others may have low levels. Some adolescents struggle with their sexual identity. This struggle is often seen in adolescents who disclose having temporary same-sex and bisexual attractions. These varying degrees of sexual interest illustrate that identity development in adolescence is a fluid process which involves individuals making constant adjustments.

Also important to identity development in adolescence are the key components of family and religion. Santrock (2009) reports that family can build a sense of individuality and connectedness in adolescents as they develop their identity. Santrock describes individuality as the ability for individuals to be able to communicate their unique points of view and being able to communicate how they see themselves as different from other people. Moreover, Santrock defines connectedness as the skill of an individual to respect another person's point of view which involves being open to others' perspectives. These two characteristics, which are instilled by the family, can help individuals develop a strong sense of identity.

Santrock (2009) adds that religion can be a significant factor because it helps adolescents develop their sense of belonging and purpose. Specifically, by becoming more curious about their existence, people are able to improve their spiritual identity. Santrock expounds by stating that religion has been found to impact adolescents' overall health and well-being. For instance, adolescents who are religious are less likely to use marijuana, drink alcohol, are less depressed, and are less likely to be truant from school. Santrock also found that many of these adolescents have positive peer relations, academic achievement, and self-esteem. Therefore, both family and religion are socio-emotional components that can positively affect the identity development of individuals.

In relation to Santrock's (2009) notion that religion impacts identity, my client, Marcum, experienced similar effects. Marcum is a 15-year-old African American male who suffers from depression and ADHD. On most occasions, Marcum is almost always depressed, speaking with a negative narrative about life. Divergent to his usual negative thoughts, I notice that Marcum will express positive ideologies about life every time he participates in a religious experience (e.g., reading the Bible or attending church). After these religious experiences, Marcum is always full of energy and enthusiasm. His attitude about life changes instantly, especially his newfound positivity for attending school regularly and taking his medication every day.

Marcia's Four Statuses of Identity can be applied to describe the various changes in identity development seen in many early adults (20 through 30 years of age). Santrock (2009) reports that many college students have the status of identity diffusion (i.e., having not experienced crisis or made commitments to an identity) whereas others are categorized as having an identity foreclosure status (i.e., having made a commitment to an identity but not having experienced a crisis). Even more so, Arnett (2000) and Santrock both depict that individuals in their early adulthood seek out careers while developing economic independence – cornerstones to identity development with early adults. Both authors state that early adults begin the process of selecting a mate and tend to become more family-oriented.

As well, Santrock (2009) and Arnett (2000) describe how identity development in early adulthood can be one of confusion and exploration. The authors identify how individuals at this age are more self-focused and carry with their spirit a sense of opportunity. On the other hand, Santrock explains that although early adults have full-time jobs, are college graduates, and have psychological and social competence, many of these adults move back in with their parents because of the unstable United States economy. Santrock and Arnett's information illustrates how identity development is a sinuous process that involves an individual's desire and struggle to be autonomous.

In middle adulthood (40 to 60 years of age), Santrock (2009) asserts that individuals expand their personal and social involvement and their accountability. These individuals are more attuned to maintaining a satisfactory career. Santrock describes that middle adults seek to leave something significant behind for the next generation. The author expresses this sense of legacy as generativity (described by Erick Erikson). As outlined in Santrock, Erikson defines generativity as an adult's desire to leave behind a legacy for the next generation. These legacies can include adults having offspring and leaving behind cultural remnants for the family. This ideology of legacy in middle adulthood shows how identity development consists of a sense of self-worth and belonging.

Identity development in late adulthood (60's or 70's) further supports the notion that identity is a fluid process. Santrock (2009) explains that adults in this phase of the lifespan begin to review their life's worth and value. Adults begin to adjust to new social roles and diminishing health. Santrock reveals how Erikson's theory of *integrity versus despair* (the eighth and final stage of development) plays out in this lifespan phase. Santrock states,

> This stage involves reflecting on the past and either piecing together a positive review or concluding that one's life has not been well spent. Through many different routes, the older adult

may have developed a positive outlook in each of the proceeding periods…the older adult will be satisfied (integrity). But if the older adult resolved one or more of the earlier stages in a negative way…the total worth of his or her life might be negative (despair). (p. 589)

Akin to Erikson's late adulthood phase, my late adulthood mentee named Lorenzo illustrates the tenets of this stage. Lorenzo is an African American male born and raised in San Francisco, California. Currently, he is a student at City College of San Francisco and lives alone in a single-room apartment in the city. Lorenzo's life story is composed of determination, resilience, and sadness. His resilient attitude towards a life-changing event (i.e., his positive outlook) is what impresses me the most about his personality.

For instance, when Lorenzo was 38 years of age, he was involved in a life-threatening motorcycle accident that burned 85 percent of his body. When Lorenzo wears tee shirts, I can see the pink-colored scar tissue that covers his scarred arms and shoulders. The motorcycle accident had inflicted him with a traumatic brain injury, otherwise known as TBI. Immediately after the accident, Lorenzo struggled with explicit and implicit memory loss.

What excites me about Lorenzo's perception of his accident is his positive attitude. During one mentoring session, I asked Lorenzo to describe how he maintains balance in his life. He expressively stated, "…I maintain balance through prayer and spending time with my family…and being around people that I love… I feel like I need to balance my life more by having people in my life who give more to me than take from me…" (Lorenzo, personal communication, November 20, 2010). Lorenzo's statement about balance allowed me to observe the resilience in his personality. Lorenzo has overcome a tremendous amount of pain that has allowed him to become self-determined.

Erikson's theory emphasizes how the cumulative effect of our lived experience can impact identity development in late adulthood. My initial research on identity development over the lifespan reveals that identity is a fluid process with many components that can be altered over the lifespan. Some of these components include awareness of identity, experimentation, autonomy, self-worth and belonging, and lived experiences. In this next section, I will explain a few essential characteristics to Black identity development, particularly as it pertains to Black males.

Cultural Response to Identity

Ethnicity adds to the variability of identity development in adolescence. Santrock (2009) reveals that many adolescents often feel they have to choose between their own culture and that of mainstream America. Many of these adolescents resolve their cultural confusion by choosing a bicultural identity. By this means, they identify with their culture in some ways and with the mainstream culture in other ways. Santrock defines the importance of acculturation and its effects as,

> First-generation immigrants are likely to be secure in their identities and unlikely to change much....Second-generation immigrants are more likely to think of themselves as "American," possibly because citizenship is granted at birth...For non-European ethnic groups, racism and discrimination influence whether ethnic identity is retained... Researchers are increasingly finding that a positive ethnic identity is linked to positive outcomes for ethnic minority adolescents... (p. 388)

Santrock's (2009) observations of how ethnicity impacts identity illustrate that identity development can be constructed differently in various cultures. Most significant, Santrock's information that obtaining an ethnic identity can have positive results for adolescents is equivalent to the results derived by other researchers (e.g., Merriweather-Moore, 2004; White & Cones, 1999; Wilcox, 1971; Wilson, 1991). All of these researchers found that when Black men grounded themselves in their ethnic identity (Black culture) they were able to cope with institutionalized racism and discrimination.

Similarly, in describing the maintenance of culture with immigrant families, Suarez-Orozco (2004) concludes that maintaining contact with one's culture is essential to understanding one's existence. The author emphasizes, "In order to maintain a sense of affinity with one's culture of origin, sustained contact is required. Regular visits back to the homeland in what is described as a transnational existence – facilitates maintenance of the parent culture" (p. 178). For instance, throughout my years of practice, many of my Mexican K-12 students often visit with their families in Mexico during the school year to maintain their familial connections and cultural heritage.

As described in Santrock (2009), Marcia's statuses of adolescent development are important for understanding the development of adolescent Black males. I propose that adolescent Black males commit to an identity early in their adolescence because of the many crises they endure, such as institutionalized racism, which occurs often in the public schools. Case in point, which will be elaborated further in a subsequent chapter, San Francisco Unified School District has a history of promoting institutional racism in some schools. In 1978, the San Francisco branch of the National Association for the Advancement of Colored People (SFNAACP) and a congregation of Black parents filed a class-action lawsuit against the San Francisco Unified School District (SFUSD).

Also known as *San Francisco NAACP v. San Francisco Unified School District (1978),* the parents claimed that SFUSD practiced racial discrimination and maintained a segregated school system, in defiance of the constitutions and laws of the United States and California. Claimants demanded that the school district be desegregated immediately through a court-ordered sanction and desegregation plan. The action was allocated to the Honorable William H. Orrick, Jr., who supervised the case for almost all of its nearly 30-year history *(San Francisco NAACP v. San Francisco Unified School District, 2005).* For these reasons, many adolescent Black males achieve identity (i.e., identifying as a strong Black male) because they endure institutionalized racism and discrimination.

To underscore the inadequate education of Black males, the Schott Foundation (2008) reports that in 2004 Black males from California graduated at a rate of 55 percent compared to a 76 percent graduation rate of White males. In 2005, Black males from California graduated at a rate of 54 percent compared to a 75 percent graduation rate of White males. These statistics, similar to Horn (2010), are appalling yet realistic for many young Black males who attend public school in California. Research from the California Department of Education (2008) shows in the 2008-2009 school year Black males had a high school dropout rate of 12 percent compared to a 10.7 percent dropout rate for White males.

Comparably, for the 2007-2008 year, Black males had a 12.9 percent high school dropout rate compared to a 10.3 high school dropout rate for White males. These statistics reveal that Black males in the SFUSD have an arduous challenge in the near future to embark on regarding the attainment of their high school diploma and improvement in their overall education. This evidence of Black males' inadequate education gives further credibility for the reasons why some Black males achieve identity in the early stages of their adolescent development. As outlined earlier, Santrock (2009) explains that in Marcia's Four Statuses of Identity, an adolescent classified in Identity Achievement has both endured a crisis and is fully committed to an identity. Many of these Black males have endured crises and thus commit to being strong Black males during the adolescent lifespan phase of development.

In the same way, the identity achievement status of these adolescent Black males can be seen in the lives of five mid-adult Black males as told from their personal narratives in *Voices of Successful African American Men* (2004) written by Dr. Lois Merriweather-Moore. Each of these individuals explain how they survived white

America by using their commitment, life choices, obstacles, and cultural pride as effective coping strategies - concepts of identity described in Santrock (2009).

For example, in discussing success and maintaining identity Mr. Jones, a research participant in Merriweather-Moore (2004), asserts "...this thing you call success, I don't own it, because I didn't do it by myself. I got extraordinary help from largely African Americans in support along the way...I was supposed to be assimilated, and I never did that...and I'm still Black..." (p. 65). This insight by Mr. Jones specifies how he maintained his identity while at the same time attaining success within a predominantly white society – through assistance from his Black culture.

Wilcox (1971) explains Black identity development by arguing that schools, churches, and organized groups (e.g., Black fraternities and sororities) have been most influential in developing Black identity. These organizations allowed Blacks to practice the democratic process of leadership when white America rejected them from their organizations.

Another component to Black identity development is the engagement in one's own cultural identity. Identity immersion can have positive effects on Black males' self-esteem (Merriweather-Moore, 2004; Santrock, 2009; White & Cones, 1999; Wilcox, 1971; Wilson, 1991). One example of identity immersion is the Afrocentric curriculum I use to teach my Black male students Black history. I believe my Afrocentric curriculum is effective because it gives Black males a voice and increases their self-esteem. The curriculum that I use in my tutoring is important to me because I believe that in order for Black males to be successful in school, the curriculum must reflect their culture and give them voice.

Long ago, Black males had a voice of strength, courage, and determination in Africa. Merriweather-Moore (2004) claims "...the African man had a strong sense of self, self-worth, and manhood before he was brought to the Americas. In his own country, the

African man had a voice and knew his success" (p. 15). It is my hope that by understanding their culture in Africa, Black males, through their increased cultural awareness and the cultural pride that usually accompanies the research of one's culture, will find their voices within American classrooms.

Likewise, my Afrocentric curriculum is important because I include within it many examples of the victorious men and women who dominated Africa. Merriweather-Moore (2004) proclaims "...African American men in their own country had built empires and were known and honored throughout the ancient world speaks very clearly to them being more than meager chattel when they were brought shackled and chained..." (p. 15). I believe that the cultural relevance that is infused in my curriculum will inevitably enhance the self-esteem of Black males, and by so doing, increase a positive identity within every Black male I educate.

Similar to the components that make up identity mentioned earlier by Santrock (2009), there are many mechanisms to Black identity development. In this section I have reviewed just a few including: (1) being grounded in ethnic culture, (2) acquiring identity achievement in adolescence (as outlined in Marcia's Four Statuses of Identity), (3) using Black culture as a coping mechanism, (4) becoming involved in Black organizations, and (5) becoming immersed in Black identity. I will now conclude with an overall summary of my response.

Summary

Identity is a fluid process involving multiple features that are reconstructed and reevaluated across the lifespan. The bulk of identity development occurs in adolescence with multiple experimentation phases. Identity is then reevaluated and transformed in later life as individuals continue to posture themselves within the framework of the larger society. Identity development over the lifespan indicates that identity is a fluid process that includes various mechanisms, such as testing, independence, sense of worth, and life experiences. Identity development in the Black culture is more externally forced development caused by institutional racism and discrimination. Three essential fundamentals to Black identity development involve a firm grounding in Black culture, adolescent Black identity achievement, and Black identity engagement. Thereby, I continue to propose that identity development is fluid and occurs in a different way among diverse cultures and individuals.

CHAPTER 2

THE EFFECTS OF INDULGENT PARENTING ON THE LIFESPAN DEVELOPMENT OF BLACK MALES

I first became intrigued with indulgent parenting and its effects on young Black males after reviewing the research data from Horn (2010). While reviewing my researcher journal, I noticed a consistent theme of what I subsequently termed excessive coddling between my research participants and their caregivers. After further investigation into my field notes, I noticed this type of behavior, which I currently name indulgent parenting, tended to have various damaging effects on the lifespan development of Black males.

Therefore, in this chapter, I will: (1) provide a definition of coddling and indulgent parenting, (2) discuss examples of indulgent parenting demonstrated by my clients, (3) argue the effects of indulgent parenting on normal child development, (4) reflect how counselors might deal with this issue, and (5) summarize my response. I suggest that indulgent parenting can have detrimental effects on normal child development of young Black males. This type of parenting style can restrain a child's ability to achieve individual responsibility that is essential in early childhood, middle and late childhood, and adolescence as defined in Santrock (2009).

Definitions of Coddling and Indulgent Parenting

The Oxford Dictionary and Thesaurus (2002) defines the word coddle as "…treat as an invalid; protect attentively…pamper, baby, cosset, mollycoddle, indulge" (p. 144). Similarly, the American Heritage Dictionary and Thesaurus (2005) describes the word coddle as "…To treat indulgently; baby" (p. 144). By discussing coddling, I hope to provide a lucid picture of the type of indulgent parenting I observe in my educational consulting.

Santrock (2009) discusses that indulgent parenting is a style in which parents are over-involved in their children's lives, but rarely set limits and boundaries for their children. These types of parents let their children do whatever they want, often resulting in a lack of self-control from the children. Consequently, these children "might be domineering, egocentric, noncompliant, and have difficulty with peers…" (p. 258). This definition of indulgent parenting illustrates the type of parenting style I have observed in my practice. This parenting style is entwined with coddling as explained above.

Examples of Indulgent Parenting

Several caregivers of my research participants in Horn (2010) were candid about demonstrating some form of indulgent parenting, that is to say excessive coddling. By excessive coddling, I mean acts of unrequited favors, treats, and excuses demonstrated by the caregivers of my research participants. Some of these favors offered by these parents have included providing their sons with expensive cell phones, luxurious name brand tennis shoes, excessive junk food, and unlimited video games. Because of this excessive coddling, I have observed many young Black males disrespecting their mothers verbally by yelling, cursing, and demonstrating some form of disobedience.

The main form of disobedience that I have observed from the Black males in Horn (2010) pertains to disinterest in education - not turning in school and tutoring homework, being truant, and fearing or hesitating to complete difficult assignments. For instance, one of my students, Leshawn, has been excessively coddled by his mother. When I first met Leshawn several years ago, he was in the fifth grade. During our tutorial sessions, I noticed that Leshawn would often complain when we attempted minimum amounts of homework.

When I consulted Leshawn's mother, Ms. Bowie, about his behavior she was truthful about spoiling him. She explained, "Dr.

Horn, I spoiled Leshawn because I had no choice… His father left us when Leshawn was an infant and he became my best friend…" (Ms. Bowie, Researcher Journal, January, 2009). Because Leshawn was not given boundaries and limits, Leshawn has become disobedient and indifferent towards school. In consequence, Ms. Bowie's indulgent parenting caused Leshawn to become incapable of accepting individual responsibility.

Another example of indulgent parenting occurred between my client Jeremiah and his mother Ms. Jamestown on several occasions. Jeremiah is an adolescent male who is currently in his last year of high school. After developing a personal relationship with Jeremiah and Ms. Jamestown, I recently consulted with Ms. Jamestown about Jeremiah's behavioral changes. Ms. Jamestown confided in me that Jeremiah had been spoiled as a baby. Similar to Leshawn, Jeremiah's father was absent and Ms. Jamestown was addicted to crack cocaine when he was born.

When I investigated the roots of Ms. Jamestown's coddling, she informed me that she believed her spoiling made up for the time lost between her and Jeremiah. As infants, Ms. Jamestown had to surrender both of her children, Jeremiah and his older brother, to child protective services until she recovered from crack cocaine addiction. Akin to Leshawn, Jeremiah would demonstrate signs of lacking independent responsibility in regards to his education. He refused to complete chores around the house, declined to wash his own clothes, was excessively tardy to class, and failed to complete homework assignments. When I talked with Ms. Jamestown about her excessive coddling she stated, "Dr. Horn… I know I spoiled my boys… I know I did… I gave them boy's money, I wash they clothes... I cook for them…they don't have to do nothing…" (Ms. Jamestown, Researcher Journal, June, 2009). By this means, Jeremiah lacked independent responsibility because of his mother's indulgent parenting style.

Both Ms. Bowie's and Ms. Jamestown's indulgent parenting styles (i.e., their lack of setting boundaries) have affected their children's normal lifespan development, in that neither of these young Black males have learned individual responsibility. Both parents failed to realize the privileges they provided for their sons did not match the responsibility they should have requested. This issue of indulgent parenting on Black males is particularly important because of the disproportionate number of Black males who live in poverty, the increasing rise of Black single parent families, high death rates of Black males compared to their white male counterparts, and declining academic improvements in Black males' education (Horn, 2010; Kunjufu, 2005; Losen & Orfield, 2002; McGoldrick, Giordano, Garcia-Preto, 2005; Noguera, 2008).

Effects of Indulgent Parenting on Normal Child Development

I postulate that indulgent parenting can subdue a child's ability to achieve individual responsibility that is essential in early childhood, middle and late childhood, and adolescence. However, it is important to note that I am not using indulgent parenting as a psychological tool for assessment and diagnosis, but rather as a framework to explore the effects on normal child development, or to be precise, on young Black males. For example, Santrock (2009) discusses that when a child develops personality, the infant develops a sense of self in the second year of the lifespan and independence is a central theme in a child's life.

Santrock further discusses the importance of independence by stating that "a child goes through a separation and then an individuation process. Separation involves the infant's movement away from the mother. Individuation involves the development of self" (p. 189). In the case of Leshawn and Jeremiah, because they were not allowed to experience the separation and individuation processes, they are unable to perform individual acts of responsibility. For example, completing and submitting their homework assignments.

Furthermore, Santrock (2009) divulges that separation and individuation helps to build a child's mental and motor skills. When a parent does not allow a child to choose a meal from time to time or pull the wrapper off the toilet paper, then a child can develop an extreme sense of shame and guilt for not being able to display self-control. Because the parent has hurried to every need of the child, the child has not been allowed to develop a personal sense of individuation. Because Ms. Bowie and Ms. Jamestown did not allow their sons to develop the individuation phase of development, Leshawn and Jeremiah may be suffering from shame and guilt over not being able to control themselves.

More specifically, indulgent parenting can affect a child's normal development. Santrock (2009) reports that during early childhood young children (ages infancy to 5) become self-sufficient and learn to take care of themselves. They develop skills that prepare them for school and discover how to follow instructions and identify letters. Indulgent parenting can negatively impact this stage of development because this parenting style does not allow children to cultivate autonomy. In the case of Leshawn, his developmental phase of autonomy was severely impacted by his mother's excessive coddling. She intervened in every step of his development; thereby stifling his sense of independency and self-sufficiency.

In middle and late childhood, Santrock (2009) discusses that children in this stage (ages 6 to 11) learn how to grasp the fundamental skills of arithmetic, reading, and writing. The child's sense of achievement and degree of self-control increase. Indulgent parenting can suppress this stage of child development. Both Leshawn and Jeremiah struggle with their sense of achievement and self-control in that they are unable to comprehend achievement because their mothers have always provided them with unnecessary privileges without matching responsibilities. As a consequence, their mothers' coddling warped their sense of comprehending individual achievement. Most notable, Leshawn and Jeremiah have low reading, writing, and math skills.

In adolescence, Santrock (2009) instructs that youth in this stage (ages 10 to 12 and ending in 18 to 21) are growing physically at a swift pace. There are increases in height and weight gains followed by the pursuit of autonomy and personal identity. Indulgent parenting can negatively affect this growth by not allowing children to develop their sense of independence, which has a direct link to their personality development. Indulgent parenting, in my examples of excessive coddling, has suppressed the independent development of the young Black males described in Horn (2010).

Similar to the research participants in Horn (2010) and my current caseload of clients, I find that most Black males are excessively coddled by their mothers. In the case of Leshawn and Jeremiah, their adolescent stages were stagnated because of their mothers' inability to allow them to cultivate their own independence. Because Jeremiah has already reached his adolescent stage of development, he is in constant flux about his identity. As a result, his mother's indulgent parenting has caused him to become even more confused during this time of irregular testing of identities.

To further complicate matters of normal child development, I argue that indulgent parenting can be particularly damaging to young Black males, especially regarding their academic development. As stated earlier, Santrock (2009) asserts that children in middle and late childhood should be able to comprehend the basic skills of reading, writing, and mathematics. Many of the Black males with whom I work fall well behind their peers in all areas of their basic skills. Research on the inadequate of education of young Black males in the United States including excessive special education placements, low graduation rates, and institutionalized racism in public schools elucidates my argument (Kunjufu, 2005; Losen & Orfield, 2002; Noguera, 2008).

Similar to Leshawn and Jeremiah is the case of Adrian who was excessively coddled by his mother. I worked with Adrian for approximately one year, through the duration of his fourth grade, and found some shocking depictions of coddling during the daily sequence of his life. Adrian was nine years of age when I first began to work with him and his mother. In the course of our mentoring sessions, I noticed that Adrian would consistently complain about reviewing or attempting a one-page school or tutoring homework assignment. After many conferences with his mother and other school and community members, I found a pattern of excessive coddling that was persistent in Adrian's life.

During one conference Adrian's mother, Ms. Johnson asserted, "Dr. Horn…it's my fault (voice becomes loud)….me and my momma (Adrian's grandmother) spoiled him…I know we spoiled him…I can tell by the way he talk crazy to us sometime (i.e., referring to how Adrian comfortably curses at his mother and grandmother)…" (Ms. Johnson, Researcher Journal, August, 2009). Because Ms. Johnson exceptionally spoiled Adrian after infancy, he was not shown appropriate boundaries and limits and therefore became uncaring towards his school assignments and mother. Hence, he developed a disrespectful attitude at an early age as a normal part of his lifespan development.

Losen and Orfield (2002) indicate that many Black males are excessively placed in special education and often labeled as mentally retarded more than their white counterparts. Kunjufu (2005) reports that Black males have the lowest chances to be placed in an inclusive classroom and the highest chances to be placed in separated or isolated environments regarding the placement process of special education. This imbalanced placement is partly due to what Kunjufu observes as institutionalized racism. These statistics help clarify the imbalance of educational achievement among Black males in public schools.

Most disturbing was the overwhelming perception among educators that most Black youth will fail in the United States. Noguera (2008) describes,

…the normalization of failure on the part of Black males is equally pervasive. This is undoubtedly because many educators have grown accustomed to the idea that a large percentage of the Black male students they serve will fail, get into trouble, and drop out of school. Such complacency is present not only in large urban school systems…but in more affluent suburban schools as well. (p. xix)

More explicitly, Noguera (2008) further delineates the problem of inadequate education within the context of the California schools he visits by reporting that Black youth, when compared to their white counterparts, fall considerably behind them in both standardized tests and grade level. Noguera also illustrates that teachers from the urban schools he visits often complain about lack of discipline among their students and astutely observes that the majority of the teachers who complain are white and a majority of the students in these classrooms are Black.

If indulgent parenting among Black males is not addressed by social workers, mental health workers, and educators, many of these young Black males who are categorized as special education and low achieving will be further restrained and held within these systems. Because of the lack of individual responsibility and autonomy they have not been allowed to cultivate, Black males lack the effort and the individuation that accompanies educational success in normal child development. Counselors and therapists can assist Black families by understanding the history of Black people, using the extended family in the therapeutic process, and understanding the impacts of racism and discrimination on the Black family.

Within these interventions, counselors may be able to restore the individuation and autonomy processes that are critical to normal child development. Thus, young Black males can harness their newly developed individuation to become responsible for their academic achievement, that is to say completing homework assignments and setting goals that will allow them to complete high school and attend college.

How Counselors Can Assist with Indulgent Parenting

Counselors can assist with indulgent parenting within the Black family in several ways. First, counselors must be aware of the comprehensive history of the Black family. Even though many of the clients whom I have mentioned are single parents, they exhibit strong kinship and cultural ties that are unique to the Black family. It is imperative that counselors become aware of the rich history of Black people prior to their insertion into America. The Diaspora of the Black family is rooted in their ancestral lineage of living as Kings and Queens throughout all of Africa. This reverent style of living was abruptly ended when their homelands were savagely divided by European, Portuguese, and French invasion (Bennett, 2005; McGoldrick et al., 2005). Understanding the history and incorporating it within the counseling of single Black mothers who demonstrate indulgent parenting can serve as a very important resource.

The rich history of Black families may help young Black males visualize their ancestral lineage by learning about great African leaders, such as Shaka Zulu of the Zulu nation who led an entire African empire as a strong independent African man. Shaka Zulu was raised by his mother, as a single mom, and Shaka ruled an entire nation constantly fighting off British influence. Shaka Zulu never compromised himself and his culture and he never accommodated white people. It is apparent from the literature in Bennett (2005) that Shaka's mother did not demonstrate indulgent parenting towards him. The story of Shaka Zulu and other great African Kings can be retold, in the African style of storytelling, as a therapeutic intervention – exemplifying a strong Black male who existed pre-invasion.

Furthermore, counselors must understand that although an increasing amount of Black families are becoming single parent households, networks of extended family members aid in support (Hines & Boyd-Franklin, 2005; Sue & Sue, 2008). Sue and Sue

(2008) discuss that "an extended family network…provides emotional and economic support….the rearing of children is often undertaken by a large number of relatives, older children, and close friends…" (p. 332). Similarly Hines and Boyd-Franklin (2005) reveal "A genogram can aid the therapist in gathering information about relationships and the roles of different family members" (p. 89). The extended family is a key component in understanding the complexity of the Black family structure. Counselors should inquire about the role of the extended family in each individual situation. These family members may be able to help aid in a co-facilitative solution to remedy indulgent parenting.

The Black church has always played a pivotal role in the development of Black males. Counselors should be aware that Black pastors can significantly influence the individuation and identity development processes that are essential to Black male development. Sue and Sue (2008) discuss the importance of churches by stating "A pastor or minister can help create sources of social support for family members….programs for the enrichment of family life may be developed jointly with the church…" (p. 336). Therefore, the Black church can help advise these single Black mothers with effective parenting techniques that teach young Black males how to become individually responsible.

Counselors must also understand the degrees of cumulative racism and discrimination on the Black family. Sue and Sue (2008) report that both racism and discrimination cause mistrust among the Black family. This mistrust has kept many Black families away from traditional counseling. An enhanced perception of Blacks' mistrust can be seen in the recent Hurricane Katrina disaster. Sue and Sue describe how Black families believed that if this disaster had occurred among a majority of white families, services would have been provided quickly. This conviction called "healthy cultural paranoia" is used as a coping mechanism among many Black families. Understanding racism and discrimination may help counselors build trusting relationships with Black families. For this reason, Black mothers may then allow counselors to delve more deeply into the reasons for indulgent parenting, which can usually cause shame and embarrassment among these mothers.

Summary

Indulgent parenting can curtail the normal identity development of children, particularly as it pertains to individual responsibility. For young Black males, the issue of indulgent parenting not only hinders their normal child development, it significantly stifles their academic development.   Many young Black males are categorically labeled as special education and low achieving, falling behind their white peers considerably in education (Horn, 2010; Kunjufu, 2005; Losen & Orfield, 2002; Noguera, 2008). Addressing the effects of indulgent parenting on Black males may be able to lessen some of their academic failures. As Santrock (2009) discusses, indulgent parenting can cause children to become disobedient, overbearing, self-centered, and have difficulty establishing friendships.

Therefore, the vestiges of indulgent parenting can cause young Black males to become both socially and academically immobile because they are unable to form their own boundaries. Their exposure to excessive coddling has limited their ability to understand self-achievement and identity, thereby lessening their chances of academic development. By understanding and becoming aware of the complexity of the Black family, comprehending the importance of the extended Black family, and becoming aware of the institutionalized racism and discrimination on the Black family, counselors may be able to create a holistic solution to remedy the indulgent parenting that occurs in some Black families.

CHAPTER 3

IMPROVING CHILD AND PARENT INTERACTIONS THROUGH THE STEP PROGRAM FRAMEWORK

In this chapter, I provide grounded research on child-rearing techniques for parents who would like to become knowledgeable about effective parenting modalities. Specifically, I include my observations of four different child-and-parent interactions in a natural setting and provide an alternative solution for each interaction. Each summary includes a written account of what I observed as a representation of Dinkmeyer's (1996) "four goals of misbehavior," which include attention, power, revenge, and inadequacy, as outlined in his STEP program.

STEP

The Systematic Training for Effective Parenting (STEP) program was developed by psychologists Don Dinkmeyer, Sr., Gary D. McKay, and Don Dinkmeyer, Jr. STEP is a parent education program that provides strategic parenting skills for those parents who encounter difficult behaviors from their children. STEP is grounded in Adlerian psychology and encourages a more family-involved process by nurturing responsibility and independence in children, enhancing parent-child communication, and helping children learn from the natural processes intrinsic to their self-choice. Although STEP was designed for families with typical parenting challenges, it is predominantly suited for families of children with mental health issues.

Attention

Dinkmeyer (1996) explains that attention can be displayed either actively or passively. An active form of attention can be demonstrated by children as interruption or horseplay. A passive form of attention can be displayed by children as overlooking chores. Both active and passive forms of attention seize parents' attention through the act of misbehaving.

Observation.

I observed the misbehaving act of attention between a friend and her nine-year-old daughter playing at Golden Gate Park in San Francisco, California. As my friend chatted with another colleague, her daughter belligerently interrupted their conversation. I noticed that my friend became agitated as her daughter persistently shouted "...what are we doing next mom..." All of a sudden, my friend quickly lashed out in anger at her daughter to "shut up!" I realized at that moment, my friend's daughter gained the attention of her mother through "active attention" seeking (Dinkmeyer, 1996, p. 42).

Alternative Solutions.

Upon observing this interaction, I reflected on how my friend could have addressed this situation in a different way. Dinkmeyer (1996) postulates that when a child is using active attention, parents should not give attention on demand. Hence, a rapid response from a parent fulfills the child's desire for attention. Instead, Dinkmeyer (1996) instructs parents to distract themselves during these altercations, as he writes, "When your feelings are strong, think about something else...You could think back to a good time you've had with your child...Fold laundry. Walk around the block. Look at a magazine" (p. 38).

Following Dinkmeyer's (1996) reasoning therefore, it would have been more constructive if my friend would have looked serenely at her daughter and waited until she politely asked for her attention. Once her daughter asked politely for the next plan of the day, my friend could have thanked her daughter for demonstrating patience. Subsequently, my friend could have regained her composure to explain the remaining plan of the day in a calm voice.

In the same way, Siegel and Hartzell (2003) advise parents to terminate interaction with their children when emotions become elevated. The authors write, "…The best thing to do if a parent becomes aware of her intense anger and aggressive behavior is to stop interacting with her child. Until a parent has calmed down, the situation will probably get worse" (p. 159). My friend could have de-escalated herself (e.g., breathed deeply or looked away) prior to engaging with her daughter. This would have generated a more peaceful response and perhaps a more constructive interaction.

Power

Dinkmeyer (1996) observes that some children believe they exist to be in charge. These children are persistent at taking control – the objective is to attain power. The author further proposes that children who seek this type of attention usually provoke feelings of anger from their parents. The author states, "If the parent fights the child, the child fights back. If the parents give in, the child has won the power struggle and stops misbehaving" (p. 12).

Observation.

While waiting to tutor one of my clients, I observed what I assessed as power being used in an interaction between my client and his grandmother. My client Kenyan argued with his grandmother (Ms. Jaresse) about not wanting to be tutored. As they exchanged several disrespecting phrases, Ms. Jaresse looked perplexed by Kenyan's abusive language. Kenyan had taken control of the moment by throwing a tantrum. He refused to be tutored and thus controlled the situation through his outburst.

As I waited until the altercation subsided, Ms. Jaresse became infuriated, looking at me with embarrassment. As Ms. Jaresse yelled at Kenyan "….stop acting like a fool in front of Dr. Horn…," Kenyan looked away with anger. This interaction continued until Ms. Jaresse had finally walked out of the room stomping furiously downstairs -

leaving the dispute unresolved (Ms. Jaresse, Researcher Journal, July 1, 2011).

Alternative Solutions.

Phelan (2003) explains that the goal of an intervention technique called 1-2-3 Magic is having your children "… (1) learn to think and (2) take responsibility for their own behavior" (p. 25). Equally, Phelan discusses that parents should use the 1-2-3 or counting method as a form of controlling a child's misbehavior. The system includes informing your child that they have a chance to recoup their composure. The parent of a misbehaving child holds up one finger and then two fingers and counts aloud "1 and 2."

Next, after waiting at least five more seconds, the parent holds up three fingers and says "3." Subsequently, the two chances allow children to gather themselves emotionally. If they are unable to calm their emotions and behavior, the parent issues the third count of 3 as a means to issue a consequence, usually in the form of a standard time-out (Phelan, 2003, pp. 26-27). In this manner, to thwart Kenyan's use of power, Ms. Jaresse could have refused to fight with Kenyan by withdrawing from the "power contest" and using 1-2-3 Magic - immediately ending any excess communication. Consequently, 1-2-3 Magic would have extinguished Kenyan's misbehavior of power.

Correspondingly, Dinkmeyer (1996) suggests, "…Listen to how your voice sounds. If you need to, take a deep breath. Speak calmly and respectfully" (p. 38). By following this advice, Ms. Jaresse would have also de-escalated the situation by speaking with Kenyan in a passive voice instead of yelling.

Revenge

Dinkmeyer (1996) explains that revenge involves a child's decision to get even with a parent, particularly when the child wants to "…be the boss but can't win in a power struggle…" (p. 12). Furthermore, Dinkmeyer (1996) terms "active revenge" as children being consistently offensive, saying hurtful things, and being aggressive.

Observation.

I observed revenge between a child and his mother one weekday evening on Haight Street in San Francisco, California. The parent (unidentified Caucasian mother) was giving some instructions to her child as he yelled aloud "no…I don't want to…" (unidentified Caucasian child, Researcher Journal, June 19, 2011). As the mother continued to give instruction which included redundant statements like "can you please stand up" the child continued to yell aloud and shake violently back and forth.

Throughout this 5 minute incident, the child continued to grapple with his mom by yelling aloud "…no… I don't want to…." Each time the mother issued a command, the child raised his voice louder, even shouting slanderous comments to his mother. The incident reached an apex when the child shook his mother so hard he pushed her away in a manner that made her fall back.

Alternative Solutions.

In this particular case, the mother should have avoided wrestling with her child. For example, I noticed as she tried to physically manage the child, he became more infuriated. To minimize the physical altercation with her child, the mother could have loosened her restraint with her child. Her tense body language may have added to his physical resistance. Dinkmeyer (1996) instructs parents to watch their body language by checking themselves, posing questions such as "Are you leaning in too close to your child? Does your body feel tense? Again, take a deep breath and relax your body" (p. 38).

Additionally, this parent could have used the 1-2-3 Magic system to issue a very specific directive - ending all communication until her child regained composure. Phelan (2003) teaches that parents should minimize excess verbiage when giving instructions to their children, especially with 1-2-3 commands.

More specifically, this mother could have allowed her child to experience his emotional outburst without involvement or interaction until he appeased himself. In this way, the mother could have issued her son a boundary by informing him to stand up and walk when he was ready. This approach would have also reflected Siegel and Hartzell's (2003) idea that, "Allowing your child to have his distress without trying to punish him or indulge him can offer an opportunity to learn how to tolerate his own emotional discomfort" (p. 190).

Inadequacy

Dinkmeyer (1996) describes inadequacy as a way for children to make people (i.e., adults) "… leave them alone. When the child gives up, the parent feels like giving up too…" (p. 13). The author tells that the act of inadequacy is usually displayed by children in certain areas of their life such as sports, schoolwork, and other activities. When inadequacy is being demonstrated by children, they are trying to present their faulty belief which states, "…when I try to do something and fail, I don't belong" (p. 25).

Observation.

In a separate altercation with my client Kenyan and Ms. Jaresse (mentioned above), I witnessed a display of inadequacy. As I waited one evening for Kenyan to prepare for tutoring, he began to engage in his typical forms of misbehavior. After Ms. Jaresse engages in a 3-5 minute dialogue of pleading with Kenyan to prepare for tutoring, Kenyan responds "…I'm not going to tutoring anymore…" Ms. Jaresse then mumbled in a low voice, "…well…you don't have to go if you don't want to…you're the one wasting Dr. Horn's time…" (Ms. Jaresse, Researcher Journal, June 29, 2011).

Kenyan's demonstration of inadequacy allowed Ms. Jaresse to "give in" to Kenyan. The end result was that they both exhibited uncaring attitudes toward tutoring and Kenyan's behavior elicited the desired attention from Ms. Jaresse. Kenyan's portrayal of inadequacy influenced Ms. Jaresse into pitying him.

Alternative Solutions.

One way of managing Kenyan's misbehavior was for Ms. Jaresse to terminate her discussion immediately. This ceasing of communication, as described in Phelan (2003), would have helped to distinguish Kenyan's attention-seeking by diminishing the conflict (i.e., the feedback loop). Klann (personal communication, July 5, 2011) discussed that parents and clinicians should avoid the feedback loop with children. The feedback loop involves the back-and-forth of verbal exchanges that does not lead to conflict resolution. For example, if a child yells loudly in an argument and the parent feeds into this exchange by yelling just as loudly as the child then the child has essentially won because this exchange results in a self-defeating battle (L. Klann, personal communication, July 5, 2011).

Another way of handling this situation would have been for Ms. Jaresse to encourage Kenyan through an enlightening dialogue about the importance of cooperation. She could have encouraged Kenyan to work with me (his tutor) by describing the elements of cooperation and how it can help him succeed in school and personal life. Dinkmeyer (1996) explains to parents to "....Show them (children) how to cooperate with other people. In this way, they can be a part of things and can be helpful to others too" (p. 26).

Correspondingly, Ms. Jaresse could have encouraged Kenyan by discussing African American pride. Horn (2010) discusses the significance of using Black history when giving instructions to young Black males as a means of instilling inspiration and self-importance. In this case, Ms. Jaresse could have told the story of Shaka Zulu, as mentioned in Chapter 2, and how he became a great warrior while being trained by powerful African leaders of the Zulu nation.

In my professional experience with young Black males, I often use Black history interwoven within my instruction as a means of keeping them on task and focused. Many of the young Black males listen keenly as I discuss how Harriet Tubman and others tutored slaves as a way to educate them about their rights as human beings. In this way, Black history becomes an effective tool to administer instruction and discipline while increasing their knowledge of their cultural selves (Horn, 2010).

Conclusion

Dinkmeyer (1996) and Siegel and Hartzell (2003) highlight the salience of self-reflection on the part of parents as a tool for promoting effective parenting. The incidents described in this chapter are a testimony to this idea. The forms of misbehaviors mentioned here can often be managed effectively with specific boundaries and limitations. Dinkmeyer (1996) teaches that before parents decide how to manage their child's misbehavior, they must learn to manage their own responses. For example, Dinkmeyer (1996) advises that parents should learn to think about negative circumstances in a reasonable way. The author also advises parents to review their own belief systems by examining any illogical principles they may be attached to. The author believes that parents' irrational belief systems can cause difficulties and restrict their ability to be happy. Inevitably, parents' unhappiness will inhibit their ability to parent effectively.

It is important to note that in the case examples above, the parents could only administer what they felt was appropriate correction for that particular time on that particular day. Siegel and Hartzell (2003) remind parents that "…We, just like our children, are doing the best we can at that point in time and like them we are learning more respectful ways to communicate…" (p. 187). Effective parenting is therefore a fluid process and not a linear one that is to be mastered and completed. It is important to remember that parenting decisions are not made in a vacuum and they are context-driven and subjective. From the perspectives of Dinkmeyer (1996) and Siegel and Hartzell (2003), effective parenting is forever being adjusted and improved as parents transition into new levels of human development.

CHAPTER 4

THE RIGHT TO EDUCATION: CASE STUDIES OF INADEQUATE EDUCATION FOR AFRICAN AMERICAN STUDENTS

The lifespan development of many young Black males includes a continual history of inadequate education. In my professional opinion, this history constitutes a human rights violation. The following chapter outlines the deplorable history of how young Black males, including my students, are educated in the United States.

My study of human rights education, the personal stories of my interviewees, and the *Brown v. Board of Education* (1954) case reveal that it is important to continue the fight to eliminate inadequate education for African American students and to promote the awareness of inadequate education as a relevant human rights issue. Therefore, it is hoped that my personal involvement, this literature review, and my pedagogical plan add to the continuous body of research on human rights education and stimulate the need for further research on how to increase the awareness of inadequate education, considering *Brown v. Board of Education,* violations of Article 26 of the Universal Declaration of Human Rights, and the right to education for African American students, particularly in urban areas of the United States.

This chapter provides (1) an introduction of my reflections concerning inadequate education of African American students and my research with one-on-one tutoring that support my rationale for this topic, (2) a comprehensive research section which includes a succinct literature review about research links to the violations of Article 26, research on the *Brown v. Board of Education* (1954) case, and a conglomeration of case studies of inadequate education for African American students that highlights the violations of Article 26, and (3) a pedagogical section which includes a lesson plan that promotes the awareness of inadequate education, the *Brown v. Board of Education (1954)* case, and Article 26.

Introduction

Article 26 of the Universal Declaration of Human Rights (UDHR) stipulates

> Everyone has the right to education. Education shall be free...shall be directed to the full development of the human personality... promote understanding, tolerance and friendship among all nations and all racial, ethnic or religious groups... Parents have a prior right to choose the kind of education that shall be given to their children..." (Weissbrodt, Fitzpatrick, Newman, Hoffman, & Rumsey, 2001, p. 28)

This significant article, ratified by the United States in 1992, was passed as an international law by the United Nations. It is important to my research because it provides the lens that I will use to critically evaluate the history of inadequate education for African American students.

My Reflections on Inadequate Education

I have expressed this need for adequate education, underscored by the UDHR, for years by advocating that schools be more vigilant in increasing the competence among educators by improving cultural awareness training among teachers and informing parents of their rights. For instance, as a one-on-one tutor, I work with hundreds of young Black males, ranging in age and grade levels. This tutorial relationship includes four hours of one-on-one tutoring every week for each student, observations in their classrooms, and continuous dialogues with both their parents and teachers.

Whenever I attend a class to observe my students, I take copious notes regarding my students' behavior and their teacher's pedagogical style. After observing and talking with teachers in general, I find that most of them lack cultural awareness, exacerbating the continuing problem of inadequate education among my students and other Black males in their class. In addition, I often discuss with teachers the importance of using culturally related materials and pedagogical styles that reflect the culture of most African American students within their classrooms, including the understanding of Black English Vernacular (BEV). Their responses in many of our dialogues usually have entailed the need for teaching the standards required by the school district.

As a result of these teachers' inflexible attitudes to become culturally knowledgeable, I concluded that some teachers do not believe that understanding culture is necessary for increasing the effectiveness of education among African Americans and other students of color. This lack of understanding African American culture is a violation of Article 26 because it clearly states that "education shall be directed to the full development of the human personality...it shall promote understanding, tolerance and friendship among all nations, racial or religious groups..." (Weissbrodt et al., 2001, p. 28). By downplaying the significance of culture as an important value in education, children's personalities and understanding can be damaged because of this lack in cultural awareness demonstrated by some teachers.

My Reflections as a K-12 Teacher

This research on inadequate education has caused me to reflect on both my past and current involvement as a teacher in the San Francisco Bay Area. For example, when I taught K-12, I was caring, concerned, and effective. Many of the Bay Area schools where I have taught have always been diverse. Although my class sessions were not always picture-perfect, I made an effort to improve the culture and communication of my students and colleagues within every school where I taught. As a teacher, I constructed well planned lessons that included multiple opportunities for students to express themselves. My lessons included group work, reflective writing, and individual presentations which involved rap, poetry, acting, etc. Often, I made weekly phone calls to parents to discuss the positive attributes of their children.

In addition, I often talked with the teachers to discuss resolutions for the achievement gap among the students of color. I now realize that this effort has to be manifested on a daily basis and is a key component missing in most teachers' practice. It is important for teachers to increase their efforts toward finding solutions to student achievement. This solution-oriented effort by teachers will inevitably lead to decreasing the gap between the classroom and the community because the students will be able to feel included in the classroom. In so doing, their efforts may help decrease the inadequate education practices that occur in some schools within the San Francisco Bay Area.

My work as a K-12 teacher has focused my efforts on the importance of informing parents about the achievement gap that exists. Informing parents is one of the most important elements in decreasing the gap in education among students of color because being informed will allow parents to become motivated for their children. Article 26 articulates that "Parents have a prior right to choose the kind of education that shall be given to their children…" (Weissbrodt et al., 2001, p. 28). As a result of my activism, a number of parents of the low-achieving African American students have become more involved in their children's education.

My Reflections on One-on-One Tutoring

Because of my newly inspired focus on human rights, I have increased my efforts as a one-on-one tutor. For example, I have educated children on human rights advocates, mainly the work of Martin Luther King Jr., Ella Baker, and Malcolm X. Many of my students have performed poems and written pieces that detail the work of Martin Luther King Jr. and how he helped promote justice and equality for all mankind. These video performances have been recorded and downloaded so that they can add to a continuous educational portfolio that I have been constructing for them since the establishment of our tutorial relationship.

Some of these documents include a personal curriculum, a family/ language tree (inspired by my professor Dr. Susan Katz at the University of San Francisco, California), video presentations, and other curriculum that catalogue their educational experiences. It is hoped that this portfolio can be used to reinforce the importance of their own education and inspire family members, friends, and community members on the importance of receiving adequate education.

Research

My research on inadequate education indicates that a lack of education among African Americans has been recognized as a violation of their civil as well as human rights. I begin this section with an elaboration of inadequate education as a human rights issue, relating previous research of inadequate education for African American students with Article 26 provisions. I then discuss some case studies of the remedies that had been attempted to mitigate this scourge of inadequate education historically and more recently; particularly the case of *Brown v. Board of Education (1954)*. I also include potential remedies that have emerged through case studies of my personal experience in one-on-one tutoring of African American males. I conclude this section with implications for the future.

Article 26 Violations: Previous Research on Inadequate Education

Ladson-Billings and Tate (1995) write that current realistic expressions of African American culture in schools often reduce them to unimportant examples and artifacts of cultures, such as eating ethnic or cultural foods, singing songs or dancing, reading folktales, and other less than educational presentations of the fundamentally different origins of knowledge. Their research is vital to educators because it outlines the historical trivialization of African American history that has been taught throughout public schools.

Ladson-Billings and Tate's (1995) research on African American lack of cultural representation in public schools is a violation of Article 26, which challenges "education …shall promote understanding, tolerance and friendship among all nations, racial or religious groups…" (Weissbrodt et al., 2001, p. 28). Ladson-Billings and Tate's article is associated with Article 26 in that they believe in the promotion of cultural accuracy among all students. By making all people aware of the degradation and indecencies that African Americans have received within the United States, the authors' research helps expose inadequate education as a relevant human rights issue.

Banks (2005) argues that multicultural education should incorporate and accept all students regardless of their race and cultural individuality. He also states that the challenge faced by multicultural education is to delineate how to help children from various groups negotiate the differences between the cultures of their home and community and that of school. He believes that students should acquire the information, outlook, and ability needed to function successfully in each cultural setting.

Bank's (2005) research is important to educators because it shows how the lack of cultural awareness in school is in violation of Article 26, which says "education shall be directed to the full development of the human personality and to the strengthening of respect for human rights…" (Weissbrodt et al., 2001, p. 28). Banks' beliefs are aligned with Article 26 in that he stresses the need for education among all youth, regardless of cultural background. Educators can use Bank's information to help further give support that inadequate education among African American students is a relevant human rights issue.

Article 26 Violations: Remedies for Inadequate Education Case Studies

Case Study #1: Brown v. Board of Education (1954)

The historical context of African Americans prior to Brown.

Prior to the well-known *Brown v. Board of Education* (1954) case was the renowned *Plessy v. Ferguson* (1896) case. In 1892 Homer Plessy, a citizen of Louisiana who was one-eighth black and seven-eighths white, was placed under arrest for riding in a white-only car during an intrastate trip. The event had been planned by a group of renowned African Americans from New Orleans – mainly Creoles, or French-speaking people of mixed ethnicity. Their ride was a direct confrontation of the Louisiana statute requiring railway companies to provide separate and equivalent lodging for whites and blacks. The constitutional issue in discussion was the right of a state to make and implement this kind of racial discrimination. Prior to this case, Louisiana, along with other southern states, passed white supremacy laws, which extended from the private to public realm under state mandate and enforcement (Martin, 1998).

In 1892, the Supreme Court defended these laws including those of the Louisiana Jim Crow railway statute. This decision declared that separate and equal provisions for blacks and whites were consistent with the equal protection clause of the Fourteenth Amendment. The decision also represented race as a normal, not random, classification for the description of state-defined rights (Martin, 1998). Eventually, *Brown v. Board of Education* (1954) overturned this racist law.

Mendez et al. v. Westminster School District of Orange County et al. (1946).

The case that helped support Thurgood Marshall's fight in the *Brown* case was the *Mendez v. Westminster* (1946) case. The case centered on a young girl named Sylvia Mendez who was refused entrance into an elementary school in Westminster School District, located in Orange County, California. This was a class law suit filed on behalf of all Mexican or people of Latin descent. The school districts involved were Westminster, Garden Grove, El Modena, and the Santa Ana City schools, all located in Orange County, California (*Mendez et al. v. Westminster School District of Orange County et al.,* 1946).

The grievance, founded upon the Fourteenth Amendment to the Constitution of the United States, charged that a determined policy and design of class prejudice against persons of Mexican or Latin descent and the removal of elementary school age children by the schools mentioned above are direct violations of equal protection under the law. The plaintiffs alleged that the school districts had practiced discrimination by implementing racist policies that directly resulted in the denial and removal of all Mexican children and all children of Latin descent from their public schools. This case is important to my research because it validates that segregation has detrimental effects on the overall educational development of a child which may inexorably lead to the damaging of the "full development of the human personality" as assured in Article 26 of the UDHR.

The legendary case.

On May 17, 1954, the United States Supreme Court ruled on *Brown v. Board of Education* – one of the most famous American law cases. The courts ruled that segregating children by race violated the Equal Protection Clause of the Fourteenth Amendment, regardless of the physical facilities and other elements of the schools. The case overturned the doctrine of separate but equal schools as unconstitutional. The decision reversed the Court's 1896 decision in *Plessy v. Ferguson,* which had sustained the concept and practice of state-endorsed racial discrimination, otherwise known as Jim Crow – the illusion of separate but equal public accommodations and organizations for blacks and whites.

The *Brown v. Board of Education* (1954) decision was a conclusion of joint and individual efforts waged by Blacks and a series of legal efforts by the National Association for the Advancement of Colored People (NAACP) from the early days of its existence in the 1910's and 1920's (Martin, 1998). This case is important to my research because it illustrates that inadequate education of African American males has always been pervasive. Segregation is a violation of Article 26 which articulates, "Education shall be directed to the full development of the human personality and to the strengthening of respect for human rights…" (Weissbrodt et al., 2001, p. 28).

Because African Americans were not allowed to attend school with whites, their human rights were violated because of the psychological humiliation that segregation caused. Gordon's (2006) research points to the fact that 50 years after the United States Supreme Court ruling making segregation illegal, most Black children attend public schools where they represent the majority of the student body; thus segregation still prevails today.

The limitations of Brown v. Board of Education (1954).

The continuing unresolved effects of *Brown* (1954) are powerfully expressed in Gloria Ladson-Billings (2004) keynote address during the American Educational Research Association (AERA) conference. The author points out that the ruling gave birth to specific limitations that have affected the educational achievements of Blacks ever since. She contends that the decision helped to reinforce white supremacy throughout education. For example, as the case was being argued, the author reveals that most of the litigators involved in the case discussed the case on the basis of Black inferiority, leaving the impression that Blacks were inferior to whites as opposed to fighting the case with the language of injustice surrounding segregated schools.

Ladson-Billings (2004) also argues that by addressing the issue of segregation solely on the basis of racial inferiority, the litigators and courtroom counsel helped to further pathologize Blacks as inferior subjects, a tendency that permeates in current educational values. Ladson-Billings' (2004) argument is essential for my research on inadequate education as a relevant human rights issue; the context of inadequate education must be explained thoroughly in order to fully understand its origins.

This issue of inferiority that Ladson-Billings asserts is another violation of Article 26, which declares "Education shall be directed to the full development of the human personality and to the strengthening of respect for human rights…" (Weissbrodt et al., 2001, p. 28). Because African American students were not seen as ordinary human beings, their human rights are violated because of the psychological damage that occurs when the label of "inferior" is placed upon them by many whites both within and outside the school district.

Brown's effect on Black males.

Duncan (2005) states that educational reports from Canada, United States, and the United Kingdom consistently conclude that Black males' overall academic achievement is worsening in public school. Black males make up over half of the suspension, special education, and expulsion cases in both urban and suburban areas. The author claims that the *Brown* decision was not advantageous for Blacks because the original idea of desegregation was based on a mathematical formula – desegregated schools plus integration equals harmony. This is insidious to think that by simply desegregating public schools, one would eliminate the racist, prejudicial, and heartless principles that exist in public schools today and historically.

This information is imperative to my research because parents, teachers, and administrators need to be aware that *Brown* (1954) has not remedied the inadequate education of Black students. Having discussed only one step that dealt with alleviating the problem of inadequate education historically, this next case deals with a more recent example of the same.

Case Study #2: San Francisco NAACP v. SFUSD (1978)

As introduced previously, in 1978, the San Francisco branch of the National Association for the Advancement of Colored People (SFNAACP) and a congregation of Black parents filed a class-action lawsuit against the San Francisco Unified School District (SFUSD) otherwise known as *San Francisco NAACP v. San Francisco Unified School District* (1978). The parents claimed that SFUSD, its board constituents and its superintendent, the California State Board of Education and its associates, the State Superintendent of Public Instruction and the State Department of Education were all practicing racial discrimination and maintaining a segregated school system, in defiance of the constitutions and laws of the United States and California.

Consequently, the claimants demanded that the school district be desegregated immediately through a court-ordered sanction and desegregation plan. The Honorable William H. Orrick, Jr., supervised the case for almost all of its nearly 30-year history. This history is important to my research because parents, students, and teachers need to be informed of the legalities around their local school districts. Thereby, San Francisco residents may be motivated to monitor any illegal and inadequate practices of education by the SFUSD *(San Francisco NAACP v. San Francisco Unified School District, 2005)*.

A lengthy historical analysis was articulated all throughout the *San Francisco NAACP v. San Francisco Unified School District* (2005) case. The case revealed that during a national era of widespread *de facto* segregation, if not *de jure* segregation, San Francisco faced a situation comparable to that of many other large urban school districts: its schools were divided based on race. In 1970, 63 of 96 elementary schools were segregated. At those schools, one racial group encompassed over 50% of the school population at a time when the largest racial group (i.e., white students) comprised only 34 percent of the entire elementary school student body. There were 29 predominately white schools, 23 predominately Black schools, four

Hispanic schools and seven Chinese schools *(San Francisco NAACP v. San Francisco Unified School District, 2005).*

Case Study #3: My Work with Terry

My work as a one-on-one tutor has enabled me to promote adequate practices of education and the importance of human rights. Terry, age 10, was born and raised in the Hunter's Point district of San Francisco, California. I have a personal connection with both Terry and his neighborhood because most of the children that I work with live in this community. Although this community has undergone years of tragedy, it is well known for the overwhelming migration of African Americans who fled the south to look for jobs during World War I.

My observations of Terry occurred periodically within his middle school classrooms. During these classes, Terry has been subdued at times because of the lack of appropriate pedagogical techniques, which without a doubt has caused his reading skills to diminish. For example, during one of my visits to Terry's classroom, I observed Terry playing an unrelated computer game. After inquiring about this observation, the teacher informed me that this was a technique that he used for those he deemed as the "good students." I was infuriated by this pedagogical method because Terry was reading below a second grade level.

It is important, especially for Terry's teachers, to focus any available instructional time on the goal of increasing his reading proficiency. After conducting a meeting about Terry's Individualized Educational Plan (I.E.P.), the members of his I.E.P. team were informed of this teacher's mediocre action. Since this meeting, the school has done nothing to either improve the teacher's training or support Terry's reading improvement. This lack of effort from Terry's school is in violation of Article 26 that denotes, "Education shall be directed to the full development of the human personality and to the strengthening of respect for human rights…" (Weissbrodt et al., 2001,

p. 28). Because of this lack of effort by Terry's teachers, the development of his personality may be delayed.

In addition, the lack of involvement on the part of his teachers has had a tremendous effect on both Terry and his Uncle Joe. His uncle has informed me that he has also observed Terry's teachers performing minimally during class. On many of his school visits, Uncle Joe observed the teachers placing Terry on the computer after completing a simple kindergarten assignment – an assignment far below Terry's capabilities. His uncle informed the teachers that he wanted them to challenge Terry with reading assignments that will develop his reading skills, but the teachers informed Uncle Joe they do not have the appropriate resources. I tutor Terry twice a week and our tutorials are intense. During every tutorial session, I read aloud and practice writing and vocabulary with Terry. He enjoys reading books because he consistently asks to read aloud from his book selection during the reading section of tutoring.

The emergent theme evident in Terry's story is the need for parental involvement. It is critically important for parents to require school districts, teachers, and community members to become actively involved in their children's education because inadequate education will eventually occur on some level. Smiley (2006) states that everyone should read to their children every day. I agree with Smiley because I have for many years encouraged parents to practice reading, writing, and math with their children. This daily practice of basic academics along with consistent involvement may decrease the practices of inadequate education that still occur in many school systems.

One of the most enjoyable lesson plans that I was able to work with Terry on was a human rights lesson. During this lesson, I informed Terry about the educational rights that were taken away from Blacks during and after slavery. We discussed the right to education, as declared in the UDHR, and how it is important to obtain an education, particularly due to the fact that it has not always been given to Blacks. For over a week, I talked with Terry about how Martin Luther King Jr. and others helped bring about justice and equality to many human beings, not just Black people. I also informed Terry that Dr. King was an important person to the civil rights cause because he helped raise awareness of the practice of inadequate education as a global issue.

Terry exhibited his understanding of human rights and Dr. King in a short video presentation about Martin Luther King, Jr. Terry was excited and engaged during the entire presentation while presenting his information in a confident and professional manner. I admire Terry's self-confidence and zealousness towards tutoring because he is always prepared for tutoring and eager to learn. Although he continues to struggle with reading, one-on-one tutoring has been able to increase his love for reading by consistent practice and visits to book stores and libraries.

My work with Terry and his Uncle Joe has been extremely helpful in providing a criterion that would help parents assess their child's educational environment. Both Uncle Joe and Terry's human rights are violated when the SFUSD does not advocate for his educational needs because Article 26 spell outs that "Parents have a prior right to choose the kind of education that shall be given to their children…" (Weissbrodt et al., 2001, p. 28). It is important for school districts to help parents with any areas concerning the educational achievement of their children.

Because Terry's school did nothing to enhance his educational environment, Uncle Joe is unable to provide the type of education that is necessary for Terry to achieve. Terry's school took that away because of their lack of effort. This information has added to the further justification that inadequate education is a relevant human rights issue that needs continuous monitoring and parent involvement in order to be eliminated.

Case Study #4: My Work with Jeremiah

Jeremiah is another one of my students whom I see at least twice a week for one-on-one tutoring. He was also raised in the Hunter's Point District of San Francisco, California. After dialoging with Jeremiah's teachers about the dichotomy of his behavior, being boisterous among friends and silent in the classroom, I have gained a broader perspective on Jeremiah's issue – a disconnect between the classroom and the community. This disconnect is revealed in my work with Jeremiah, indicating that there is a lack of understanding of Jeremiah's culture, a lack of expression by Jeremiah, and a lack of imagination from Jeremiah's teachers to find new ways to engage Jeremiah.

I have observed Jeremiah using Black English Vernacular (BEV) on many occasions. My observations of Jeremiah occurred in his science class and at recess. I noticed that Jeremiah was nervous during my visit to his science class in particular. It appeared that I have a positive effect on his life as his tutor/mentor, and that he really values our relationship. All of his teachers appreciated my visit and his foster mom continues to encourage my visits to his school. Most significantly, I observed that Jeremiah was comfortable and relaxed when he was with his friends (the homies) at recess and throughout lunchtime using BEV fluently.

On the other hand, in his regular classroom he was quiet and tranquil. He often looked nervous while staring haphazardly at the clock, waiting conspicuously for the bell to ring. This bothered me intensely because I have known Jeremiah for years and I have never seen him this reserved. This observation as well as my research have driven me to pursue this notion of bridging the gap between the classroom and the community of African American students who use BEV.

There is a lack of universal multicultural sensitivity among Jeremiah's teachers. For example, I have often discussed with his teachers his use of BEV with his friends and his quietness in the classroom. During these discussions, his teachers were amazed at both my observations and my profuse notes. The teachers appeared to have no consciousness about Jeremiah's use of language. For example, as I discussed the cultural significance of BEV, the teachers seemed uncaring about this cultural reality. Their responses to my questions regarding their knowledge of African American history and multicultural education reflected their adaptation to the current education standards in which they had to teach.

Thus, their indifferent demeanor allowed me to take a step back and reflect on the bigger picture behind Jeremiah's issue. I could now see why Jeremiah had been a different person in class than at recess and home. For that reason, Jeremiah's teachers may not believe that learning about the use of BEV and other cultural realities regarding multicultural communication is necessary for their classroom instruction. This lack of understanding is a direct link to the lack of teacher training that school districts need to address.

Unfortunately, Jeremiah's teachers remain satisfied with teaching a standard curriculum for the district and for their own personal convenience. Their lack of cultural sensitivity and awareness is a violation of Article 26 which asserts "Education ...shall promote understanding, tolerance and friendship among all nations, racial or religious groups, and shall further the activities of the United Nations for the maintenance of peace......" (Weissbrodt et al., 2001, p. 28). Jeremiah's understanding and tolerance is weakened when his teachers refuse to become culturally aware and informed.

Additionally, this perception of societal knowledge has helped me gain more understanding as to why teachers have no urgent reason for including the knowledge of multicultural consciousness within their pedagogy. When teachers do not apply the knowledge of multicultural communication within their pedagogy, cultural miscommunications often occur. In Jeremiah's case, he and his fellow students are not able to include their culture because his teachers are culturally uninformed. Jeremiah's teachers failed to teach the common awareness of culture to their students, which is implied by Article 26. This research on Jeremiah serves as another example of inadequate education for African Americans validating these inadequacies as a human rights violation.

Case Study #5: Boys of Baraka

This movie, by directors Heidi Ewing and Racheal Grady (2005), provides an example of how a non-government organization (NGO) attempts to mitigate the problem of inadequate education for African Americans within the Baltimore School District. The film states that 76% of Baltimore's African American males fail to graduate high school. The movie portrays a program named Baraka School, a boarding school in Kenya, East Africa, where each year 20 at-risk African American males are chosen from the Baltimore public schools to attend the Baraka School for two years. The film zeroes in on a group of four boys from Baltimore (Richard; 13 years old, Romesh, Devon; 12 years old, and Montrey; 12 years old), who travel 10,000 miles away from home to pursue a better education.

During their first year at the school, the boys tried to balance the natural beauty of rural Africa and the urban life of the ghetto that they had left behind in Baltimore. Far away from the violence and other dilemmas that 12-year-old boys should not have to worry about, they all excelled in their educational pursuits. As the year progressed at the school, they learned to problem solve cooperatively. Because of the Baraka program, the boys' self-esteem improved, grades improved, and possibilities for attending a high-performing high school were increased.

At some point in the program, the director of the program articulates her thoughts to the boys by informing them that some of the African American boys, who had previously graduated from the Baraka School, have successfully graduated from high school – keeping in mind the 76% failure rate that had previously existed. Additionally, the program offered these Black males a different perspective and outlook on their education. It allowed them to glance into the educational environment of other cultures, particularly Kenya, Africa.

After a successful year at the school, the boys return home for a summer vacation. During this period, the boys struggle to integrate back into their environment. At the end of the summer, the administrator of the program informs them that the program has been closed due to security reasons caused by conflict in the Middle East. The film then follows these boys on their journey to pursue education back home without the Baraka School support. Most of the boys do well except one – his name is Richard. Richard has always performed at a mediocre level in school. While attending Baraka, his self-esteem increased because he began to talk positively about himself and his goals in life. After the Baraka School closes, Richard struggles in a low-performing Baltimore high school. His former counselor describes that Richard may never graduate from school.

Conversely, Montrey, who is currently a freshman at one of the top-performing high schools, has become one of Baltimore's elite mathematics performers in high school. The film ends with Montrey attending a city college appreciation ceremony for all of the top scholastic performers in Baltimore. This is so powerful because the message that is unintentionally stated is that Black males can survive obstacles that may impede their academic success when given the opportunity, especially when their right to education is exercised.

Prior to the Baraka School experience, these African American boys and their parents had their educational rights violated. The schools that they attended did nothing to increase their academic skills, develop their personality or self-esteem, or allow their parents the choice to pursue high-performing academic institutions for their children. Article 26 indicates "Education shall be free...shall be directed to the full development of the human personality... promote understanding, tolerance and friendship among all nations and all racial, ethnic or religious groups… Parents have a prior right to choose the kind of education that shall be given to their children…" (Weissbrodt et al., 2001, p. 28). The film was helpful to my research because it allowed me to gain an understanding of another remedy that has helped African Americans succeed in education.

Future Implications

Smiley (2006) argues that before community leaders formulate a plan of improvement, they should collaborate with its existing leaders to properly address the issues at hand. Because of the exhausting work with my professor, my research with human rights, and my one-on-one tutoring, I am establishing an on-going collaboration process with leaders. For example, Calvin Thomas is a social worker in San Francisco, California. Calvin and I have been friends for over 20 years. He has always had a love for children and youth rights. He currently works for a nonprofit organization, which provides services to thousands of San Francisco County youth. Calvin had suggested that he would like to help collaborate with my efforts of promoting the right to education for all youth. He has specific standards that he feels should inform every parent's education of their children.

Mr. Thomas suggested that any educational organization, including schools, tutoring agencies, and mentoring agencies, should always be consistent. He explained that parents, students, and administrators have complained to him that one of the problems the school district and students face is a lack of consistency.

Mr. Thomas often uses the work that I do as a reference in his supervision meetings, and he refers most of his clients to me for tutoring. He informed me that my one-on-one tutoring is first-rate and has been more effective than his other tutors from other companies. He believes that part of the success of my work has been my organizational skills and my consistent effort along with the support that I provide to the parents, students, and teachers. He believes that in order for any program, school, or support service to be effective, consistency and longevity with the students are a necessity.

Research Stipulations

Andreopoloulos and Claude (1997) describe several responsibilities that may aid in the institutionalization of human rights education within teacher education. The authors discuss that professional preparation of teachers should be a fundamental organizing principle for educational practice. For instance, teachers must engage in a philosophical and practice-based discourse that challenges them to consider the human rights dimensions. This dialogue can help prospective teachers clarify and make explicit for themselves the values of human rights education.

Additionally, the authors claim that future teachers must develop analytical criteria by which to assess the human rights condition of a classroom and the policies and practices of a school or district. After developing standard criteria of analysis, teachers can then structure a classroom that incorporates a human rights way of life. Thus, the methodology of a human rights approach can help aid in the evaluation, grouping, teacher response, questions, and establishment of rules within the classroom. The authors' advice for making human rights a foundation for all educational establishments is imperative because it gives educators specific tasks on how to implement this procedure.

Pedagogical Tool

Social justice curriculum unit: rationale.

The following social justice curriculum unit has been constructed for an eight week intensive summer youth program hosted at a local San Francisco college campus. The purpose of this program will be to develop students' skills for college preparation and to enhance their overall awareness of recently emphasized human rights issues. The main objective of the Social Justice Curriculum unit is to improve students' comprehension regarding the historical practices of inadequate education for African American students, to identify inadequate education as a relevant human rights issue, and to increase their participation in the improvement process towards ending inadequate education both locally and globally.

This lesson will be a part of a continuing curriculum unit on human rights education. By the end of the unit, the students should be familiar with Article 26 of the UDHR, the disenfranchised history of African Americans within the United States, and the *Brown* (1954) court case and its significance as a human rights issue. The students will construct a final project that will increase the general awareness of human rights education.

The first lesson entitled SELF represents social justice because it looks at how individuals can make a difference in themselves. When people look inward before they begin to study how their outer environment affects them, they begin to face themselves in ways they may have touched on before but put aside for another time. It forces them to view and review who they are and what they stand for. I found in my work with many high school students that they are quick to judge, and rarely look at themselves first to see how they can be a part of the solution. Some students see the world as a place that should define them rather than taking an active role in defining their world.

The next lesson on FAMILY links to social justice because it looks at how youth can make a difference within their families. When youth take the step from looking within themselves to looking within their families, they can then consider how to make a change. Some youth never get a chance to look into their family history for several reasons. This assignment is one approach toward breaking the cycle of miscommunication or non-communication that occurs in most families.

The lesson on COMMUNITY is a direct connection to social justice because it looks at how individuals can make a difference in their communities. Multiple public disparities plague our communities today; therefore, students need to learn how to aggressively and professionally attack these equity issues. One simple and important way is for students to get involved within their communities. Finally, the lesson on MAKING THE DIFFERENCE helps students construct an action plan that will help the cause for social justice because their individual plans will involve the who, what, when, how, and where of students making a difference. Culturally, students will have different means to address a plan of action and implement it into their future.

At the end of the unit, students will create and present a group community awareness project (e.g., video, music, or written interview) that will represent both the knowledge they have gained from the unit and their advocacy for adequate education as a human rights issue. The final projects will be presented during the final week of the summer program.

Social justice curriculum unit: syllabus.

WEEKS 1-2: I CAN MAKE A DIFFERENCE IN MYSELF! (Unit 1)

Intro's

Reading & Writing Assignment

Movie (Boys of Baraka)

Discussions

Presentation

Resources: UDHR/ The Covenant with Black America

WEEKS 3-4: I CAN MAKE A DIFFERENCE WITHIN MY FAMILY! (Unit 2)

Reading & Writing Assignment

Library Research

Discussion

Mock Interviews

Resources: UDHR/ The Covenant with Black America

WEEKS 5-6: I CAN MAKE A DIFFERENCE IN MY COMMUNITY! (Unit 3)

Reading & Writing Assignment

Movie (Beyond Brown)

Guest Speaker

Resources: UDHR/ The Covenant in Action

WEEKS 7-8: MAKING A DIFFERENCE: A PLAN OF ACTION (Unit 4)

Reading & Writing Assignment

Movie (Malcolm X)

Plan & Practice Interviewing for Final Projects

Presentation of Final Project

Resources: UDHR/ The Covenant in Action

Final project background.

Final projects will be a combination of music, film, and writing. The students will construct a project that incorporates the UDHR laws that specify the right to education. Students will present their projects to the class as well as the entire student body of the summer program. Students can further develop their projects by making them publishable for youth magazines in both manuscript form and electronically.

Conclusion

In conclusion, the promotion of adequate education is crucial because inadequate education can have severe long term effects for both children and parents from all countries. The deprivation of adequate education may eventually lead to a lack of job opportunities, a deficiency in access to higher education, and a decrease in economic wages (Smiley, 2006). By reviewing the *Brown v. Board of Education* (1954) case and other related cases of inadequate educational practices; teachers, students, community leaders, and politicians can help understand and increase awareness of inadequate education as a relevant human rights issue.

CHAPTER 5

THE IMPORTANCE OF SPEAKING EBONICS

Included in the lifespan development of some Black males is the fundamental use of Ebonics among some young Black Males. This chapter discusses the importance of language in the lives of Black males and how understanding and awareness of Ebonics can increase validation for its inclusion in the educational system.

Black English Vernacular and Ebonics

Although Black English Vernacular (BEV), otherwise known as African American Vernacular English (AAVE) and Ebonics are used interchangeably throughout this chapter, it is important to note that there are distinct differences between these terms. Depending on the source (e.g., non-linguists v. linguists), both terms have divergent sociocultural and historical contexts (Lenahart, 2001).

Ebonics

The term "Ebonics" was first coined in 1973 by psychologist Robert L. Williams to describe certain linguistic patterns and codes that house a distinctive grammatical and lexicological base employed by some Blacks. Delpit (2002) discusses a distinctive Ebonics speech pattern among Blacks called code switching. This use is a reality of the Black community and occurs on a daily basis. Code switching happens when Blacks face a selective situation, where they have to choose between using Standard English or Ebonics. This use of code switching is a tool that allows Blacks to survive in a racist world where language can decide whether or not Blacks can become employed, for example.

Black English Vernacular

Means-Coleman and Daniels (2000) describe the history of this Black English Vernacular by suggesting that it derives from a mix of languages that stem deep from slavery. During the arrival of slaves to the Americas, the slave owners would mix the slaves so that they would not be able to speak with other slaves from their original tribe. In order for African slaves to adapt and survive, one of the strategies was to create a dialogue, which involved a creolization process. This process involved aspects of African languages which included, Hausa, Mandingo, Vai, and Wolof, all merged together with the English spoken by Southern, white slave holders. Some researchers even refer to Black English Vernacular as an offshoot of white southern English spoken primarily by Blacks from the south.

The Author's Point of View

Although there are many interpretations of the distinctions between Ebonics and Black English Vernacular (Brinson, 1998; Delpit, 2002; Delpit & Perry, 1998; Hoover, 1998; Lenahart, 2001; Means-Coleman & Daniels, 2000; Meier, 1998; O'Neil, 1998; Smith, 1998; Smitherman, 1998), these definitions and distinctions lay the foundation for the observation that some young Black males speak with a different speech pattern than their mainstream American counterparts. More significantly, as the author of this text I am by no means postulating that I am an expert in languages nor do I claim to be a linguist. I am merely arguing the importance that caregivers of young Black males understand the fundamental language of Ebonics spoken among some young Black males.

Introduction

Through their arguments, the contributing authors in the book *The Real Ebonics Debate* (Delpit & Perry, 1998) dismiss the unfounded information about the original position of the Oakland Unified School District's (OUSD) Ebonics resolution. These critical analyses lead me to believe that most public school classrooms within America use Standard English (SE) as the norm for instruction. Consequently, because this common form of teaching has not worked for most poor African American children, I believe Ebonics should be used as an instruction medium to teach African American children.

All of the authors, particularly the teachers from OUSD, support my claim based on arguments that show: (1) the ineffective use of SE within the classroom, (2) misinterpretation of Ebonics as a language, (3) linkages of Ebonics to Africa, and (4) its effectiveness within the classroom. Information on Ebonics is imperative because it validates its use as an instructional technique that can aid the education of some African American children, thereby, giving hope to teachers, parents, and administrators about future generations of African American children. Ebonics-based teaching might provide a means for reducing the exclusion of African American children from the mainstream.

Ineffectiveness of Standard English

Some authors offer successful ways of teaching SE to African American children. From her research, Delpit (1998) found that "…teachers have had students become involved with…various kinds of role-play….drama productions allow students to practice…Standard English…" (p. 20). Delpit's example points to the fact that there are some practices where instruction in SE can be effective for teaching African American children.

On the other hand, some of the teachers interviewed give reports which question the efficacy of using SE as the mode of instruction within the OUSD. For instance, Delpit and Perry (1998) state the opinion of Ms. Secret, an elementary school teacher, who has been teaching at Prescott Elementary for 30 years. Ms. Secret asserts that using SE does not guarantee that African American children will necessarily be successful in school. She purports "Children are not empowered simply because they know subject/verb agreement. That is not powerful for children if they don't have content in which to use the language" (p. 80).

Additionally, Hoover (1998) discusses that most African American children appear to lack in reading proficiency because some schools do not offer them appropriate cultural tools and testing materials that enhance their distinct abilities. She explains "…most tests are also…biased against Ebonics speakers…the competency of the African-American student needs to be measured by a variety of tests…" (p. 127). Hoover's point is significant because many African American children are stigmatized, categorized, and labeled ignorant by some teachers who ascribe to Eurocentric hegemony because they are seen as unable to "master" SE. Thus, having SE as the fundamental mode of teaching and assessment within the classroom is detrimental to a majority of African American children and leads to further subjugation of a group that is already marginalized.

Misinterpretation of Ebonics as a Language

O'Neil (1998) provides a snippet from interviews he conducted that at times contrasts the belief that Ebonics is a language. One interviewee states "…AAE (African American English)…derived from …West African languages as well as from English. West African grammatical structures are…masked by English words: a creole account…of AAE" (p. 39). This interviewee's depiction of Ebonics diminishes its validity as a language. O'Neil's interviewee further de-emphasizes Ebonics' legitimacy by positing that African American children are not predisposed to Ebonics, in other words Ebonics is not in their genes, and therefore cannot be considered a language. This ideology diminishes the authority of Ebonics as a language because it erases the roots.

In opposition, Smith (1998) dispels the popular belief about Ebonics through critical evaluations and evidence in support of the value of Ebonics. He does so through his precise explanation of Ebonics that reveals its connection to West Niger-Congo African language. According to him, Ebonics "…is not a dialect of English. The term Ebonics…refers to the linguistic continuity of Africa in

Black America" (p. 57). Smith's point helps illuminate the fact that Ebonics is a comprehensible, standard language.

Smith (1998) also suggests that white scholars do not have a "logical explanation for why, in the entire African Diaspora, there is not a single hybrid English and Niger-Congo dialect that has an English grammar as its base with African words superimposed" (p. 57). This information from Smith is extremely important because it helps eliminate the claim of most white scholars that Ebonics is a derivative of SE. This legitimacy of Ebonics as a language is critical for educators because it provides them with the validation that is needed before it can be used in the classroom as a medium of instruction.

Linkages to Africa

Meier (1998) posits that most of the teachers, whom she trains in the credential program that she teaches, begin the program with predetermined ideas concerning Ebonics. She writes that "many also brought with them negative stereotypes about the language, characterizing it…as 'slang', 'street talk', 'bad English', 'wrong' and 'not really a language'" (p. 119). Meier's teachers thereby invalidate the linkage of Ebonics to Africa by discrediting its authenticity.

On the contrary, other authors articulate the fact that Ebonics has a direct association with Africa. Smitherman (1998) discusses this historical connection through her statement "Ebonics spoken in the United States…is rooted in the Black American Oral Tradition…of African (primarily West African)…linguistic-cultural traditions" (p. 30). Smitherman thus dispels the misinformation that Ebonics has no roots - a declaration that most whites use to dismiss the authenticity of Ebonics.

Another voice that resonates with Smitherman's is Ms. Davia Dalji who is also mentioned in Delpit and Perry's (1998) book. Ms. Davia Dalji, who teaches English at Castlemont high school in the OUSD and is the national vice president of the National Association of

Black Reading and Language Development, contends that "the language is a retention of the West and Niger-Congo African linguistic structure…Ebonics is a beautiful African and Pan-African language…" (p. 115). Ms. Dalji's contention regarding Ebonics is crucial because it further confirms its linkage to Africa. When using Ebonics in the classroom, teachers should be knowledgeable of Ebonics' origin in order to properly educate African American children.

Effectiveness within the Classroom

In Delpit and Perry (1998), John Rickford, a linguist, declares that the legitimacy of Ebonics as a medium of instruction is weakened because many people have preconceived notions. These views have led to teachers being less attentive to the needs of Ebonics-speaking African American children. He says "A teacher might assume that somebody who speaks Ebonics is dumb…It's a very dangerous kind of mistake to make" (p. 62). His interpretation offers an explanation for some of the effects caused by the misunderstanding of Ebonics. These misinterpretations devalue Ebonics as a language and challenge its use in the classroom.

On the other hand, Ms. Davia Dalji (mentioned earlier) opines that using Ebonics to teach African American children can be successful within the classroom. Ms. Davia Dalji declares that using Black writers in the curriculum who employ Ebonics within their writing helps African American children distinguish between Ebonics and SE. Thus, they are able to learn SE in conjunction with their home language and not devalue it. She says "This is what I love about African-American writers. They write in Ebonics and Standard English, so students learn to translate the Ebonics to Standard English and the Standard English to Ebonics" (p. 108). Ms. Dalji's example may help teachers understand that there are precise ways to use Ebonics inside the classroom.

Hope for Future African American Children

From her research, Smitherman (1998) reveals that teacher attitudes play a significant role in providing adequate or inadequate education for African American children who speak Ebonics. She reports "Black English-speaking youngsters…are perceived to be slow learners or uneducable. Their speech is seen as unsystematic and…constantly corrected" (p. 167). Smitherman's research displays the negative perception of Ebonics, which can diminish the hope for future teachers who enter the field of teaching.

Differing with Smitherman's research, Meier (1998) counters that it's essential that educators become trained and informed so that the validation of Ebonics can be sustained within the classroom for future generations of African American children. Meier (1998) claims that education has to be rooted in the past and connected with the present in order for all children to be truly educated, especially for African American children. She also argues that teacher attitudes must change in order to facilitate Ebonics instruction within the classroom.

When talking about how she trains her teachers, Meier (1998) expounds that they must understand that "Black Language…is …constantly changing…multifaceted and multivoiced…" (p. 125). The author's position on teacher training is exceptionally valuable because some white teachers view Ebonics as a meaningless dialect of English. This ideology cannot be further from the truth. In order to effectively teach African American children, teachers must have a thorough knowledge of Ebonics. This knowledge can be gained through comprehensive teacher training.

Moreover, Brinson (1998) gives a particular use for Ebonics within the classroom. She discloses that she had grown up changing her identity to assimilate within White society. After realizing that she could not further hide from her African American culture, she returned to the classroom to teach African American children using Ebonics. She states "I might begin with a poem…written in Standard English and juxtaposing it with Black vernacular…I eventually reinvent the poem using Ebonics" (p. 135). Brinson's example is exactly what teachers need to understand. Using Ebonics accurately in the classroom can help teachers maintain its validity and longevity.

Essential to the cause of the Ebonics debate has been the program that has been used to train OUSD teachers for years - the Standard English Proficiency program (SEP). Commenting on its original intent, Delpit and Perry (1998) describe "This statewide initiative…acknowledges that systematic, rule-governed nature of Black English…this language should be used to help children…read and write in Standard English" (p. xi). The authors further explain that the OUSD's resolution enforced that all teachers become a part of the SEP program. This information is fundamental for school districts because programs such as SEP can be used as a model to help assist with the instruction of all African American children.

Although SE has been the mode of teaching in the classroom, it has failed in educating a majority of poor African American children. Information on Ebonics as a valid language has now been reported and it needs to be incorporated within the curricula. It is imperative for teachers to be trained in the language and culture of African American children in order for them to make any difference in their education. I hope that by using an Afrocentric pedagogical methodology, which includes exposure to Black writers and activities that help make a distinction between SE and Ebonics, African American children can enhance their reading and writing proficiency in SE.

CHAPTER 6

MARIJUANA ABUSE AND TREATMENT

All of the incarcerated Black males whom I counseled over the past year admitted in their intake interview that they smoked marijuana. More shocking, after my queries about their excessive use of marijuana, almost all of these young Black men disclosed that their marijuana use helped them cope with stress, increased their appetite while living on the streets, and eased the pain of trauma they experienced growing up – this is unacceptable. Therefore, in this chapter, I provide up-to-date research concerning marijuana treatment which includes: (1) a brief history of marijuana, (2) a summary of the topic, (3) a literature review, and (4) a conclusion. To supplement the authenticity of this chapter, I have inserted citations from peer-reviewed journals, books, and my personal viewpoints.

History

Insaba and Cohen (2007) state that marijuana, historically known as cannabis, was traditionally used as a source of "…oil and fiber, for its edible seeds, as a medicine, and a psychedelic…." (p. 8). Early civilizations such as Greece, Rome, and England used hemp essentially as a fiber. It was also used in prehistoric societies to help make clothing, shoes, and paper. Furthermore, the authors report that marijuana was used in many religious ceremonies and festivals among different cultures.

As civilizations advanced, Insaba and Cohen (2007) reveal that hemp, otherwise known as Cannabis, was used by new American colonies as a crop that was harvested like cotton. In fact, the authors teach that hemp was just as important as cotton – used for rope, clothing, supplies, etc. Understandably, the profitability of hemp declined after slavery ended due to costs of paying workers.

Additionally, Insaba and Cohen (2007) report that marijuana smoking was not recognized in the United States until 1910 in Texas. Insaba and Cohen illustrate how the media demonized marijuana as an evil Mexican drug. Thereby, fear and scare tactics were used to fight immigration issues in Texas during the 1900's. Correspondingly, many states fought to ban marijuana use by promoting it as one of the most dangerous drugs.

Insaba and Cohen (2007) discuss that cannabis harvesting in the United States focused primarily on the use of "…fiber for rope, paper, and oil…" (p. 22). By the 1960's, people rebelled against old beliefs about marijuana because they found it was not as demonic as it was represented by the media. Many artists, poets, and youth began using marijuana as a form of rebellion. Likewise, people began creating various techniques for growing marijuana that eventually produced a high concentration of THC (delta-9-tetrahydrocannabinol) – the main psychedelic ingredient in marijuana.

Overview

Marijuana is the most frequently used illegal substance in the United States. Sinha, Easton, Renee-Aubin, and Carroll (2003) report that there are "…approximately 5.5 million weekly users…" (p. 314). Most significant, marijuana use in young abusers (ages 18-25) can affect their health. To be exact, marijuana use among this age group can increase their health risk behaviors, depression, and abuse of other drugs (Litt, Kadden, Kabela-Cormier, & Petry, 2008). These effects will be illustrated by an individual case in a subsequent chapter.

In general, there is a lack of research on effective treatment for marijuana abuse, especially pharmacological treatment. This gap must be addressed because the number of marijuana-related emergency room visits has risen significantly throughout the years (Levin, et al., 2004).

Despite many efforts to successfully treat marijuana abuse and dependence, marijuana abstinence is difficult to attain. Some programs have tried by using abstinence-based vouchers and various other treatment techniques such as cognitive-behavioral coping skills and motivational management (Litt et al., 2008). Both Sinha et al. (2003) and Litt et al. (2008) disclose that increasing self-efficacy in marijuana abusers can lead to a reduction in overall marijuana use.

By definition, the American Psychological Association (2000) considers substance abuse to be a maladaptive pattern that is noticeable by significant difficult consequences related to continual abuse of substances. Substance abuse can cause people to fail at work and school, including neglecting their children and family. Substance abuse damages brain function, causing prefrontal cortex mutilation. Similarly, substance withdrawal involves the human body's tissue dependence on the substance (S. Garanzini, personal communication, 2011).

More specifically, the American Psychological Association (2000) reports the following information for individuals with 304.30 Cannabis dependence,

> …Individuals…have compulsive use and associated problems…Individuals with Cannabis Dependence may use very potent cannabis throughout the day over a period of months or years, and they may spend several hours a day acquiring and using the substance. This often interferes with family, school, work, or recreational activities…

(p. 236).

Thus, cannabis dependence causes individuals to be consumed by the searching, purchasing, and consuming of cannabis-related drugs.

Those who abuse Cannabis (305.20 Cannabis Abuse) may often have poor performance at work and school as well as impaired driving skills. These individuals also have legal issues that are a result of arrests from cannabis possession. These individuals tend to have family problems that are directly related to their cannabis abuse (American Psychological Association, 2000).

Literature Review

Given the above information on marijuana, three articles demonstrate positive results for treating marijuana substance abuse (Levin et al., 2004; Litt et al., 2008; Sinha et al., 2003). Sinha et al. (2003) studied probation-referred marijuana abusers. The study involved 65 marijuana-using participants who were between the ages of 18-25. The participants were recruited from a publicly funded outpatient substance abuse facility in New Haven, Connecticut.

All participants had to meet the DSM-IV criteria for marijuana abuse. Each participant was assigned to two types of three-session treatment processes in which they were evaluated for a 28-day treatment. One group was assigned to motivational enhancement therapy (MET) and another group was assigned to motivational enhancement therapy plus contingency management (MET/CM). In the MET/CM therapy, participants received vouchers for each treatment attendance.

Participants in MET treatment were subjected to what Sinha et al. (2003) describes as, "…the therapeutic stance is one in which empathy is expressed, resistance and argumentation are avoided, and self-efficacy is supported…" (p. 316). The first session involved creating a therapeutic alliance. In addition, therapists provided clients with information about marijuana abuse. The central focus of the first session was to increase participants' willingness to engage in treatment through marijuana awareness.

The second session of the MET treatment included assessing participants' motivational levels, which involved creating a change plan. During the session, the therapist and participants discussed ways to avoid marijuana use, mainly staying away from high-risk situations. If a family member attended session two, they were included in the treatment planning process. The third session in MET focused on reviewing the participants' change plans and assessing high-risk situations in the past week. Recommendations to continue treatment in the outpatient clinics were made for each participant in order to reduce marijuana use.

Similarly, participants in the MET/CM treatment received the same three-phase treatment as MET participants. Likewise, these participants received vouchers with different values as they attended each session (i.e., $25 for the first session, $35 for second, and $45 for third session). Participants also received $5 bonuses for arriving at sessions early (Sinha et al., 2003). Assessments of each participant involved a weekly interview and a post-treatment interview. Self-reporting and urine specimens were collected as data.

The results of this study revealed that participants in both treatments reported significant reductions in marijuana use and improvement in legal problems. Sinha et al. (2003) reveal that a significantly high number of participants completed the MET/CM 28-day treatment compared to the MET treatment (64% vs. 34%). These findings suggest that marijuana abusers benefit from scientifically validated treatments, that is to say MET/CM treatment.

Levin et al. (2004) studied the effects of using divalproex sodium on individuals who were deemed marijuana dependent. The overall goals of this study were to decide if patients would seek pharmacological treatment, determine if these patients could be retained in treatment using a method that was developed for cocaine-dependent users, and review if divalproex sodium could be used as an effective treatment for marijuana dependence.

This 12-week study was conducted at a New York State Psychiatric Institute in the treatment facility called the Substance Treatment and Research Service (STARS). Twenty-five participants were randomly chosen from a pool of applicants who answered advertisements in local newspapers. Some dropped out because of missed appointments. Participants had to smoke at least five marijuana joints per week and meet the diagnostic criteria for marijuana dependence. Many marijuana users who are dependent often report high rates of irritability, craving, and anxiety when they are not using.

Research on divalproex sodium (an anticonvulsant medication) has been used to treat different psychiatric conditions similar to the above mentioned conditions by marijuana dependent users (Levin et al., 2004).

Participants were given a placebo in single-blind conditions, where information is withheld from participants. Those remaining received divalproex sodium or a matching placebo. Participants were given 500 milligrams of divalproex sodium to be taken twice a day for seven days, spaced between 12-hour intervals. After the seventh day, the dosage was raised on two other occasions. Some participants' dosages were eventually raised up to 2000 milligrams. Patients who could not endure at least 250 milligrams of divalproex were eliminated from the study.

Additionally, Levin et al. (2004) report that patients were seen at the clinic twice for one-on-one relapse prevention therapy throughout the 12-week study. During their visits urine samples were collected to test the levels of tetrahydrocannabinol. A reading greater than 20 ng/ml (nanograms per milliliter) was considered positive. Clinicians also collected data from self-reporting measures which included irritability levels analyzed from the Hopkins Irritability Scale and the Snaith Irritability Scale. In addition, Levin et al. inform that "Marijuana craving, marijuana self-reported use, and psychological measures were compared for the two treatment groups using a repeated measures analysis of variance with groups (divalproex sodium vs. placebo)" (p. 24).

Survival analysis (Kaplan-Meier) indicated that there were no significant differences between the groups on treatment maintenance. There were also no significant differences between the two treatment components (administration of divaloproex sodium as opposed to placebo) in terms of either marijuana use or psychological symptoms. In spite of the treatment group, participants reported a reduction in their frequency and amount of marijuana and a reduction in irritability.

For these reasons, Levin et al. (2004) suggest that marijuana-dependent patients will seek treatment and can be adequately maintained in a pharmacologic trial.

Litt et al. (2008) studied 240 adult marijuana users for a total of 14 months. Participants were assigned to one of four 9-week treatment conditions. These conditions included case management, motivational enhancement therapy/cognitive-behavioral coping skills training (MET/CBT), contingency management (ContM) therapy, and a combined MET/CBT plus a ContM treatment. Participants' abstinence levels were the measurements studied after each 9-week treatment condition. Ninety day abstinence was recorded every 90 days for 12 months.

The participants were a diverse group of men and women recruited via newspaper and radio advertisement. The participants had to meet the DSM-IV criteria for cannabis dependence. The purpose of this study was to explore the mechanisms of treatment-related change in the use of marijuana. All treatment conditions, with the exception of ContM, were conducted in 60-minute individual outpatient sessions.

CBT, MET, and ContM are different yet they share similar mechanisms to attain treatment gains. CBT assumes that those who relapse lack the skills to effectively deal with environmental triggers. The goal of CBT is to provide clients with skills to obtain abstinence and to manage stress and high-risk situations. Litt et al. (2008) teach that "MET is a non-confrontational approach that seeks to help patients resolve ambivalence about their drug use…" (p. 639). The goal of MET is to help individuals develop the motivation to change behavior. Basically, the goal of ContM is to increase abstinence through reinforcement of abstinent behavior.

The MET/CBT intervention involved two sessions of motivational enhancement therapy followed by seven sessions of coping skills training. Litt et al. (2008) report, "…The MET component involves using an empathetic style of therapy designed to help participants resolve ambivalence, develop motivation change and set goals for behavior change…" (p. 641). CBT (cognitive behavioral skills training) focused on attaining abstinence and managing high-risk situations.

The participants in the ContM therapy received a voucher if they tested negative in the urinalysis. These participants met for 9 weeks, for about 15 minutes each session. The initial voucher rate was $10 for the first clean urine and $15 per week for each negative urinalysis. If the participant tested positive, no reward was given and the voucher was reset to $10 for the next session. The case management intervention was supportive in nature and designed to help participants with problems of daily living. To reduce overlap, MET/CBT plus a ContM treatment was employed (Litt et al., 2008).

Regardless of the treatment, abstinence was demonstrated during and after treatment. Initial abstinence was higher for those in the ContM condition but over time, the MET/CBT resulted in greater abstinence. Most significant, self-efficacy and coping skills were assessed as significant factors in increased abstinence.

Conclusion

There are limited studies on effective treatment for marijuana abuse. Research by Levin et al. (2004), Litt et al. (2008), and Sinha et al. (2003) shed light on some effective treatments for marijuana dependency and abuse. These studies comparatively reveal that pharmacology and therapy that involve motivational enhancement and contingency management can reduce marijuana use and increase abstinence. Most significant, both Litt et al. (2008) and Sinha et al. (2003) conclude that improvement in a patient's self-efficacy (i.e., mastery of a stressful situation) may lead to successful behavioral performance – management of high-risk environments or abstinence from marijuana.

CHAPTER 7

USING TRANSPERSONAL PSYCHOTHERAPY
WITH INCARCERATED YOUTH

In this chapter, I analyze an article by Himelstein (2011) regarding his use of Transpersonal Psychotherapy (TP) with incarcerated youth. To elaborate my analysis, I use scholarly research and examples from my practice as an educational consultant and marriage and family therapist trainee. This chapter is organized in the following manner: (1) an overview of the article, (2) relevancy of the article, and (3) a conclusion.

Overview

Himelstein's (2011) article describes the theoretical relevance and the author's use of TP with incarcerated youth in his practice, which is based in San Francisco, CA. Essentially, Himelstein believes that TP is the most relevant therapeutic modality for incarcerated juveniles because of five influential factors, symptomatic of this population, that TP is able to positively impact. To be exact, these factors are (a) stance on change, (b) the relationship, (c) resistance work, (d) death, and (e) worldview. Thus, because of TP's positive impact on these five concepts, Himelstein hypothesizes that TP is the most effective approach for working with incarcerated adolescents.

Stance on change.

Himelstein (2011) declares that in order to experience true change with incarcerated adolescents, therapists must understand the nature of behavior change. The author states "…The client is the human being that comes into contact with her or his authenticity with the therapist as the model and guide for that way of being" (p. 39). By this means, Himelstein assumes that incarcerated adolescents are willing to change their behavior when they do not feel forced, especially within the safety of a TP therapist-client relationship.

The relationship.

Similarly, Himelstein (2011) postulates that TP is relationship-based – the therapeutic relationship takes priority over any other method or intervention. More specifically, the author reaffirms that when a TP therapist has the ability to remain present with a client (i.e., in the moment) and establish an authentic therapeutic alliance with their clients; incarcerated youth become enthusiastic about exploring their incarceration on a more profound level.

Resistance work.

Himelstein (2011) confirms that incarcerated youth mask their feelings of incarceration in excessive amounts of humor as a way to minimize their stress. Appropriately, TP therapists do not view this excessive humor demonstrated by incarcerated youth as damaging. On the contrary, TP therapists view this behavior as "...honored mechanisms that the incarcerated clients will most likely use in between therapy sessions for their psychological survival" (p. 39). That is to say, TP therapists' positive perspective about humor as an effective coping mechanism reduces feelings of resistance towards therapy with incarcerated adolescents.

Death.

TP is effective with incarcerated youth because many of these youth experience disproportionate exposure to violence. This extreme exposure to violence increases their high-risk behaviors such as substance abuse, driving under the influence, and other thrill-seeking behaviors (Himelstein, 2011). Thus, TP therapists are aware of these "invincibility" behaviors as a form of expressing their disturbed emotions about their extreme exposure to violence. The author further clarifies, "....incarcerated youth often understand that their lives can be taken at any time under violent circumstances" (p. 40). For this reason, TP therapists help incarcerated youth unpack feelings associated with excessive exposure to violence because of the negative impact on an adolescent's worldview.

Worldview.

Likewise, constant exposure to violence and death negatively impacts incarcerated youth's worldview in that it "contributes to an unhealthy relationship to the external world." (p. 40). Specifically, the developmental phase of incarcerated adolescents (i.e., individuation) is negatively impacted because these youth see the world as an unsafe place – transporting this negative attitude into their adulthood. In this manner, TP therapists are able to challenge this negative outlook by enhancing the awareness of incarcerated youth "…in which the client relates to the outside world" (p. 41). Namely, TP therapists continuously encourage incarcerated adolescents to preserve their individuation by choice.

Relevance

Himelstein's (2011) article is exceptionally relevant to the concepts discussed in a life transitions context, particularly as it relates to meaning making, positive psychology, and normative transitions.

Meaning making.

Bussolari (personal communication, 2011) described meaning making as an individual's process of interpreting a life event. For example, when two people are in a car accident, each individual might interpret the accident differently. In the same way, TP is inherently a meaning-making modality because the overall goal is to question clients about their existence (i.e., who are we and why are we here?). For this reason, Himelstein's (2011) article is significantly relevant to the life transitions of all individuals but primarily incarcerated adolescents whose worldview of society is often impaired by excessive exposure to death and violence.

Specifically, Himelstein (2011) presents a vivid example of meaning making with his client named Alex. The two primary goals of this particular therapist-client relationship were to (a) remain present and in the moment and (b) maintain a safe environment. Prior to the session, Alex had negative thoughts about the world because of excessive exposure to violence and death. Hence, Himelstein used TP's inquisition processes with Alex to engage in profound meaning making regarding his negative worldview – resulting in the debunking of the world as unsafe.

Positive psychology.

Positive psychology involves the therapist's ability to focus on the attributes of a client. In order to facilitate this process, it is important for therapists to realize that clients need to be stabilized and to "meet the clients where they are..." (C. Bussolari, personal communication, 2011). Basically, positive psychology is used by therapists to build positive emotion, engagement, and meaning with their clients. Because human beings are wired to remember the negative, positive psychology readjusts negative thoughts (Seligman, Rashid, & Parks, 2006).

Similar to positive psychology, TP is used by Himelstein (2011) with his clients to readjust their negative worldviews and identity issues. For instance, Himelstein describes his use of TP with his client Jeremy to readjust negative feelings about being bisexual. As Himelstein and Jeremy developed a sincere relationship, Jeremy disclosed his bisexuality. Most important, Himelstein not only validates Jeremy's disclosure (i.e., meets Jeremy where he is developmentally) but inquires about Jeremy's belief that bisexuality is immoral.

As Jeremy talked more insightfully about his bisexuality, answering Himelstein's (2011) thought-provoking questions, Jeremy began to feel positive about his bisexuality. In this case, TP was used by Himelstein within the framework of positive psychology to develop Jeremy's positive emotion and meaning regarding his bisexuality.

Normative transitions.

Normative transitions are defined as anticipated transitions that happen to the majority of people – events that are expected over the family life cycle. Some examples include birth, adolescence, marriage, aging, or death (C. Bussolari, personal communication, 2011). However, I believe the lifespan development of incarcerated youth's excessive exposure to violence is indicative of a normative transition. I make this point prior to my analysis of Himelstein's (2011) article because it is important to speak to the linearism and rigidity of many family life cycles. For example, many family life cycles present distinct stages for Western families in transition that include young adults leaving home, being married, having families, etc. – leaving out developmental phases that are solely unique to incarcerated adolescent males of color (e.g., excessive exposure to violence).

Case in point, over the past 20 years as an educator and community activist I have worked with adolescent males of color, especially previously incarcerated and probationary adolescent Black males (Horn, 2010). As a result, I find that many adolescent males of color who come from underprivileged families suffer from disproportionate rates of poverty, institutional racism, and community violence (Boyd-Franklin, 2003; Himelstein, 2011; Horn, 2010; National Center for Health Statistics, 2010). Thus, I propose excessive exposure to violence is a normative transition for incarcerated adolescent males of color.

To illustrate this proposition, the case of a previous client, named DJ, whom I counseled during my traineeship, is instructive. DJ was born and raised in an impoverished Bay Area neighborhood where he observed violence every day. For example, during one of our therapy sessions DJ disclosed observing a young boy being shot in the head. DJ exclaimed "...it was trip...this dude pointed the gun at this kids head and then bam (imitating the sound of a gun)...I saw potna's head (victim) fall back...." (DJ, personal communication, August, 2011). During several therapy sessions, DJ disclosed similar incidents of violence. For these reasons, I believe excessive exposure to violence is a normative transition for incarcerated adolescent males of color that should be included in their lifespan developmental models.

Similarly, although Himelstein (2011) does not directly address the belief of excessive exposure to violence as a normative transition, the author's comprehensive data about its prevalence among incarcerated adolescent males of color validates my point. For instance, Himelstein makes numerous references throughout his article regarding the excessive exposure to violence among incarcerated adolescent males of color, especially clients from his practice. Therefore, by inferring a type of normalcy among incarcerated adolescent males of color, Himelstein supports my theory that excessive exposure to violence is a normative transition.

Conclusion

Himelstein (2011) sheds light on the importance of TP's effectiveness with incarcerated adolescents. The author posits that TP is effective with incarcerated youth because of its impact on (1) stance on change, (2) the relationship, (3) resistance work, (4) death, and (5) world view – five concepts indicative of this population. I propose that TP is effective because the therapeutic alliance allows for incarcerated adolescent clients to feel safe – ultimately disclosing personal issues and releasing suppressed emotions.

Most significant, I find TP useful as a therapist trainee because it allows me to meet my clients at their particular developmental level. Therefore, I am constantly present and in the moment with them. In this way, TP helps reduce the anxiety many of my clients (most of whom are incarcerated males of color) hold within themselves regarding their excessive exposure to violence, reoccurring incarceration, and dehumanization of being incarcerated.

CHAPTER 8

USING EXPERIENTIAL AND NARRATIVE THERAPY TO RELEASE DJ'S SUPPRESSED EMOTIONS

In this chapter, I offer an extensive case presentation of how I assessed and treated my client (anonymously named DJ). Therefore, I provide an explanation of my clinical work with DJ through the following case conceptualization lenses: background, theory, diagnosis, formulation, treatment, crisis, legal, diversity, assessment, and limitation. To enhance the validation of this case presentation, I include scholarly articles, books, and experiences from my training as a marriage and family therapist trainee (MFTT).

Background and History

My case study is of a 17-year-old adolescent Black male named DJ for whom I provided individual therapy for a total of three months as a marriage and family therapist trainee. DJ was on probation when we first began our sessions, pending judgment for an arrest for assault, but has since then been released from probation and exonerated of all his charges. In our initial intake, DJ disclosed that he frequently used marijuana. His marijuana use began at the age of 12, disclosing that he was smoking about two to three marijuana cigarettes per day.

In high school, DJ began smoking three to four marijuana cigarettes per day. When I asked him about his marijuana use, he stated "....you know...just trying to relax...you feel me...tired of everyone being on my back...my mom's sweatin' me...females trippin...." (DJ, personal communication, October, 2011). Through DJ's various disclosures during our initial intake sessions, about what he believed to be stressful events, I hypothesized that DJ used marijuana as a coping mechanism. Based on the conditions outlined in the American Psychiatric Association (2000), I suggested on his multiaxial assessment a provisional diagnosis of 304.30 Cannabis Dependence (see Table 1).

Table 1.

Multiaxial Assessment

Name	DSM Code	Disorder
DJ	Axis I:	304.30 Cannabis Dependence
	Axis II:	None
	Axis III:	Frequent Migraine Headaches
	Axis IV:	Communication Suppression Unhealthy Friendships
	Axis V:	GAF = 70 (on average)

Furthermore, DJ discussed in our later sessions that throughout his sophomore year of high school, he began smoking marijuana blunts (large marijuana cigarettes). For example, he disclosed during one session that he and his friends smoked at least five to six blunts per day. This type of marijuana use can be damaging to an individual's brain development, especially an adolescent who is still developing synaptic growth (Santrock, 2009). Thereby, DJ's numerous confessions of marijuana, social-cultural issues, and family background encouraged me to form a tentative theory that DJ used marijuana as a means of coping with unresolved emotions. I will elaborate on my premise in the following sections.

Statement of the Theoretical Model

Throughout our sessions, I used Experiential Family Therapy (EFT) and Narrative Therapy (i.e., a hybrid therapeutic approach) with DJ to release his suppressed emotions. To support my use of EFT with DJ, Nichols (2010) describes "…the root cause of family problems is emotional suppression" (p. 195). In essence, EFT postulates that healthy families should allow individuals within the family the freedom to express themselves – creating self-fulfilled individuals. By this definition, I used EFT (i.e., the freedom to self-express) with DJ to increase his self-efficacy through candid communication. Through his outspoken narrative, I wanted to co-facilitate the consideration of alternative forms of coping instead of using marijuana.

My justification for using narrative therapy, as defined in Nichols (2010) and White and Epston (1990), was to assist DJ with deconstructing his problem-saturated narrative and reconstructing a new positive-reinforcing narrative. The overall goal of narrative therapy is to deconstruct problem-saturated narratives and recreate new narratives through a dual-externalization process of (1) charting a problem's effects on the family and their relationships and (2) charting the influence of the family in the life of the problem.

Additionally, the true essence of narrative therapy occurs when the therapist helps to unite the family through a process of finding sparkling events. This process involves the therapist's inquiry of families about unique outcomes (i.e., sparkling events) as a way to elicit times of resistance and to create counterplots, which identify ways to counteract the problem if it resurfaces. The process includes describing times where this family resisted their family problem (e.g., DJ's suppression of emotions). Hence, my desire was to allow DJ to reiterate his narrative in an effort to highlight his successful attempts of coping with stressful life transitions.

Assessment and Diagnoses

In order to understand DJ's marijuana use, in the light of prevalence rates among adolescents, I will discuss research trends regarding marijuana use reduction in this section. Research on marijuana use explains that large amounts of daily marijuana use, similar to the amounts DJ used, can suppress the emotions needed from clients to engage in the healing process of therapy. To be precise, marijuana suppresses enthusiasm, effort, desire, motivation, and determination (Insaba & Cohen, 2007; Levin et al., (2004); Litt, Kadden, Kabela-Cormier, & Petry, 2008; Sinha, Easton, Renee-Aubin, & Carroll, 2003).

As identified previously, marijuana is a regularly used illegal substance in the United States. Sinha et al. (2003) report that there are "...approximately 5.5 million weekly users..." (p. 314). Furthermore, marijuana use in young abusers (ages 18-25) can affect their health. That is to say, marijuana use among this age group can escalate their health risk behaviors, depression, and abuse of other drugs (Litt et al., 2008).

To reiterate, there is currently a lack of research on effective treatment for marijuana abuse, specifically pharmacological treatment (Levin et al., 2004). In spite of many efforts to successfully treat marijuana abuse and dependence, marijuana abstinence remains difficult to attain. Some programs have tried abstinence-based vouchers and various other treatment methods such as cognitive-behavioral coping skills and motivational management (Litt et al., 2008). Both Sinha et al. (2003) and Litt et al. (2008) do reveal that increasing self-efficacy in marijuana abusers can lead to a reduction in overall marijuana use.

The abovementioned research is pertinent for understanding DJ because of the intermittent trouble that he has been involved with throughout his life, particularly the case of his previous alleged assault. This research clarifies the importance of my hybrid therapeutic method to assist DJ with releasing suppressed emotions and increasing self-efficacy. Marijuana treatment will be explained in detail in the following sections of this chapter.

Clinical Case Formulation

In order to assess DJ's marijuana use, I will be utilizing the Family Systems Perspective and several related concepts. For the most part, DJ and his two sisters were raised by his mother and father. After they divorced, DJ lived with his mother while occasionally visiting his father. The divorce, a major transition for DJ, impacted his lifespan development in that when DJ explained his occasional robberies as a teenager, I noticed that these were times where he was not currently living with his father. Thus, I predicted that his father's absence may have impacted his lifespan development in that he felt abandoned or hurt by the lack of daily access to his father caused by the divorce.

To clarify the negative impact of the divorce, DJ discussed in a session, "...sometimes when I'm with my homies...we just be bored and stuff...we just get high...we be jackin' fools and getting' high...you feel me..." (DJ, personal communication, September, 2011). Nichols (2010) discusses that part of the life-cycle notion is that families often foster problems from their transitions. In this way, DJ's marijuana use may be caused by the lack of daily presence from his father – the marijuana helps suppress his emotions over the divorce.

In yet another session, DJ discussed how he patiently attended to his grandmother and grandfather during their medical battle with Alzheimer's. DJ's love for his grandparents echoed all through his problem-saturated narrative about the thorough care he gave to them every day. As DJ described his tasks of caregiving, which included cleaning the buttocks of both grandparents after their bowel movements, I realized that their passing impacted DJ significantly. Thus, his grandparent's passing authenticated his frequent use of marijuana as a coping mechanism to manage his feelings through suppression.

Furthermore, DJ's use of marijuana as a coping mechanism can be theorized to be a result of the loss of close relationships. One relationship was taken away through divorce and the other through death. Regardless of the level of normality ascribed to these life transitions (i.e., divorce as non-normative and death as normative), DJ explained the significance of these relationships throughout our therapy sessions. For instance, when I asked about the relationship with his father, he reported "….my dad be telling me to get my stuff together…you feel me…he be telling me to get good grades so I can make something out of myself…" (DJ, personal communication, September, 2011). DJ's current intimate relationship with his father clarifies the impact of the lack of his father's daily presence in his life as a teen.

Carter and McGoldrick (1999) suggest that in order to comprehend the individual, the person's family system must be understood. The authors explain that individual development occurs in the context of significant emotional relationships within the family. In this context, DJ's relationship or lack thereof with his father and grandparents may add to his stress of development because he did not have access to his father or grandparents during pivotal points in his lifespan development. Consequently as a stress management tool he resorted to marijuana use which suppressed his emotions.

Treatment Planning and Course of Treatment

I met with DJ once a week for one hour. During our sessions, DJ was always responsive and engaging. On more than one occasion, DJ discussed concerns around involvement with the wrong crowd. I empathized with DJ's concern and praised his participation with therapy. All throughout our treatment, DJ remained engaged and participated in several clinical assessments, including the Beck's Depression Index (BDI).

In order to begin the process of developing alternative coping mechanisms, I used a narrative approach to inquire about the origins of

DJ's marijuana use. I asked DJ during one therapy session to "paint me a picture of the DJ who never used marijuana…what would that DJ look like, act like, and how would he relate to people…" (A. Horn, personal communication, October, 2011). As DJ looked at me with surprise on his face, he talked honestly about "staying focused in school" and paying attention to his mother and teachers (DJ, personal communication, October, 2011). He also mentioned on numerous occasions during his "DJ who never used" narrative that he would avoid certain friends.

As a therapeutic goal of developing alternative coping strategies, I probed deeper by asking him to elaborate on his meaning of avoiding friends. He restated, "…I mean you know…just telling folks that I'm cool off dat smoking…Imma be focused and do my thang…you feel me…just tell 'em no and keep movin'…" (DJ, personal communication, October, 2011). Afterwards, I commended DJ about having such an unwavering belief of saying no to people, even though his narrative was imagined. As a result, a narrative technique facilitated an effective coping mechanism from DJ's theoretical narrative – DJ stated that he will decline marijuana from his friends.

As therapy continued, my goal was to release his suppressed feelings regarding what I termed as DJ's feelings of abandonment about his father and unresolved grief about his grandparents' deaths. Case in point, when I delved into DJ's marijuana use, his disclosures were minimal. Conversely, when DJ did feel the need to honestly discuss the relationships with his father and grandparents, they were often positive with specific references. For example, he often talked about how his father currently scolds him for missing school or not staying out of trouble. I noticed that he smiles when he talks about his father in this authoritarian (i.e., boundary setting) parental style. Thus, I wrote in my process notes that DJ longed for his father's constant presence.

Likewise, when DJ talked about his grandparents, he often discussed their individual impact on his life. He informed me on several occasions how he loved to work at his grandfather's grocery store. He enjoyed the responsibility and the role of caregiving he provided to the customers. In the same way, his grandmother encouraged him to be thoughtful to others while she occasionally cooked traditional Black family meals for DJ.   In view of this information about DJ's family, his narrative helped reaffirm his identity within his family as (1) a doting son who yearned for the firm father he never had consistent access to and (2) the caregiving grandson who desired to take care for his grandparents who were no longer in his life.

Crisis Evaluation and Intervention

During the course of our therapeutic relationship, I found no need to assess DJ for crisis intervention. As a standard policy of the non-profit agency I work for (Youth Justice Institute), I thoroughly explained confidentiality and the limitations – given that DJ was a minor. In regards to DJ's case, at the time of our intake and through the course of therapy I assessed no imminent danger pertaining to DJ's mental health.

More specifically, DJ's marijuana use had been almost entirely eliminated from his system by the time our therapy sessions concluded. Conversely, there were a few times where I observed DJ to be intoxicated during therapy. As a recourse to his intoxicated state of mind, I reminded DJ about our agency's informed consent policies (i.e., discontinuing therapy when clients are deemed intoxicated) and subsequently ended our session prematurely. DJ appeared accepting with this organizational decision and therefore returned the following week to continue therapy.

Legal Mandates and Professional Ethics

After numerous sessions with DJ, I often reflected if I projected my involvement with violence and feelings of abandonment with my father onto DJ's case presentation. To illustrate my concern, I reflected on growing up as a young child and how I was often involved in mischievousness, including being suspended from school for fighting, street fights, vandalism, and petty theft.

After much personal reflection about my childhood, I am aware that my animosity is a direct result of the abandonment I felt from my father caused by my parents' divorce. In my case, I expressed my suppressed emotions by acting out mischievously. By this means, I was concerned if my assessment of DJ was comingled with my countertransference of abandonment from my father.

Human Diversity Issues

There are a number of social-cultural issues that impact DJ's lifespan development, for example, a lifetime exposure to violence. Over the past 20 years as a teacher, community activist, and now as an MFTT, I have worked with underserved adolescent males of color. As a result, I find that many adolescent males of color, who come from underprivileged families, particularly Black males, struggle with poverty, institutional racism, community violence, high rates of post-traumatic stress disorder (PTSD), and excessive incarceration (Boyd-Franklin, 2003; Horn, 2010; National Center for Health Statistics, 2010; Richardson, 2008; Synder & Sickmund, 2006).

Recalling DJ's previously described witnessing of a shooting as well as other incidents of violence, the effect on his adolescent development, being involved with violence, elucidates the importance of how social-cultural components of young Black males' lifespan development can directly influence their adolescence, specifically experiencing greater exposure to violence. After becoming aware of DJ's social-cultural experiences, I further speculated that DJ's desire to use marijuana frequently could be induced from his traumatic experiences of community violence. To be precise, DJ used marijuana as a coping mechanism to suppress his emotions regarding his exposure to violence.

Assessment of Outcome

In general, EFT strives to unblock suppressed emotions and communication and seeks to increase the self-esteem in individual family members. NT attempts to elicit sparkling events in order to highlight previous successes of fighting family problems. As stated earlier, even though I treated DJ as an individual client I used components of EFT and NT to help unpack the reasons for his marijuana use. Specifically, DJ used marijuana to suppress emotions regarding his father's absence and loss of his grandparents. I now propose that DJ has been impacted by my combined therapeutic approach of EFT and NT by providing a space for DJ's unrestrained self-expressions during therapy. As a result, DJ's self-efficacy has been increased through expressiveness and recreating a new positive narrative (Lawrence, 1998; Nicholas, 2010).

Limitations and Judgments

Although I enjoyed working with DJ immensely, I found myself to be overly excited during our therapy sessions. For instance, I often smiled because I was excited to be working with a Black male. I smiled on more than one occasion when DJ disclosed disturbing family issues, particularly his observations of community violence. I believe these frequent attacks of smiling were due to my excessive happiness to be in his presence – diminishing my clinical presence.

Even more, when reflecting on DJ's case, I could have reviewed his case through the lens of acute stress disorder (ASD). ASD (DSM code 308.3) is defined in the American Psychological Association (2000) as,

> …B. Either while experiencing or after experiencing the distressing event, the individual has three (or more) of the following dissociative symptoms:
>
> (1) a subjective sense of numbing, detachment, or absence of emotional responsiveness

(2) a reduction in awareness of his or her surroundings (e.g., "being in a daze")

(3) derealization

(4) depersonalization

(5) dissociative amnesia (i.e., inability to recall an important aspect of the trauma)… (p. 471).

Given this definition of acute stress disorder, DJ attributed symptoms of ASD, particularly the depersonalization of violence he observed growing up as a child. Thus, by revisiting the case with this new information, I could have unpacked DJ's depersonalization of violence in a way that could have revealed more substantial information around his emotional suppression.

Conclusion

Working with DJ allowed me to experiment with different therapeutic modalities and enhanced my self-confidence as a future therapist. Overall, I learned that the therapeutic process is in part impacted by (1) the therapeutic alliance and (2) the process after the therapy session has ended – life simply occurring to the client and therapist. My life has changed by meeting DJ because I am forever reflecting on and affected by our face-to-face interactions and conversations that occurred during our therapy sessions.

CHAPTER 9

THE PRESSING NEED FOR ACCOUNTABILITY GROUPS AMONG YOUNG BLACK MALES

In this chapter, I describe my overview, rationale, and instructions regarding a Youth Accountability Group (Y.A.G.) for incarcerated adolescent males of color. To add to the validation of my proposal, I include scholarly articles, books, and experiences from my training as an educational consultant and clinical practice as a marriage and family therapist trainee (MFTT).

Overview

There are a number of social-cultural issues that impact the lifespan development of adolescent males of color, particularly a lifetime exposure to violence. Over the past 20 years as a teacher and community activist, I have worked with underserved communities of color. As a result, I find that many young adolescent males of color, who come from underprivileged families, struggle with: poverty, inadequate resources, institutional racism, community violence, high rates of post-traumatic stress disorder (PTSD), and excessive incarceration (Boyd-Franklin, 2003; Horn, 2010; National Center for Health Statistics, 2010; Richardson, 2008).

Similarly, as a Marriage and Family Therapist Trainee (MFTT) I have worked with numerous clients who have been exposed to violence in their community as a normative life transition. As described previously, DJ, one of my clients, described how he observed a young boy being shot in the head. Additionally, during several therapy sessions DJ disclosed comparable incidents of violence. More poignantly, DJ's recurrent thoughts of violence are noticeable signs of what the DSM IV classifies as 309.81 Posttraumatic Stress Disorder. For instance, throughout our sessions, DJ relived many experiences, including several self-disclosures, about random violence that he either experienced or witnessed growing up.

97

In this way, DJ's depictions are defined in the DSM IV as, "... (2) recurrent distressing dreams of the event... (3) acting or feeling as if the traumatic event were recurring..." (American Psychological Association, 2000, p. 468).

Therefore, DJ's adolescent exposure to violence illustrates the importance of understanding how social-cultural components of adolescent males of color can directly influence their lifespan development, specifically the effects of greater exposure to violence. After becoming aware of the social-cultural experiences that many of my clients endure daily, I noticed a pattern among those who were recently released from the Juvenile Justice Center (JJC). On many occasions, these youth were re-incarcerated, exposed to more violence in their community, or immediately killed after being released shortly after incarceration (Horn, 2010; Richardson, 2008).

Although there are no national statistics on juvenile recidivism, Snyder and Sickmund (2006) report that six in ten juveniles return to prison after they are released before their 18th birthday. Most alarming, Richardson (2008) reveals that many Black males are often victims of violent death shortly after their release from juvenile prisons. As an educator of underserved adolescent males of color, many adolescent males of color disclose to me that they were fatherless – lacking comprehensive conversations that would hold them accountable during their lifespan development. As a result of this lack of accountability in their personal lives, many of my tutees and mentees allowed me to hold them accountable through our candid conversations about life skills, education, navigating institutionalized racism, and dealing with the onslaught of violence in their communities (Horn, 2010).

After years of working with underserved adolescent males of color, I began to speculate that many of these youth, some of whom were incarcerated in JJC, lacked accountability in their lives. In other words, no one significant person held them accountable for their whereabouts, goals, and professional aspirations. Aside from being provided the basic needs of shelter and food, many adolescent males of color roam the streets with no accountability or guidance for survival after being released from the JJC.

In addition, when adolescents have two biological parents to return home to after being released from prison, indicating potential for more accountability, they are less likely to engage in future criminal behavior as opposed to adolescents who return to other types of homes (Snyder & Sickmund, 2006). Therefore, the primary goal of Y.A.G. is to teach, model, and provide weekly accountability to incarcerated adolescent males of color in order to minimize their recidivism in the JJC.

Rationale

My rationale for creating Y.A.G. is to help incarcerated adolescent males of color challenge their thoughts about time and its importance in their life. As stipulated above, many adolescent males of color succumb to violence, drop out of high school, experience inadequate education, and suffer excessive incarceration. The purpose of Y.A.G. is to teach adolescent males of color how to be accountable for one another in an effort to achieve personal and professional goals. In essence, I have found that many adolescent males of color lack these specific skills, which inevitably increases their rates of recidivism in the JJC.

When tutoring and mentoring adolescent males of color, I often teach life skills that pertain to understanding the importance of time management. During a recent weekly home visit to a local San Francisco family, where I tutor their son, I disclosed,

> We (as human beings) only have 168 hours per any given week to perform our tasks that impact our progression towards human development (24 hours a day times, 7 days a week, equaling 168 total hours). We can neither add to that calculation nor repeat a particular week. We have only one

chance every week at maximizing those 168 hours to the fullest. (A. Horn, personal communication, 2012).

Thus, I often teach about the "168 hours per week" concept to underserved families and their children because I believe it is paramount that adolescent males of color hold each other accountable through accountability activities.

Furthermore, with many of the youth whom I have tutored, mentored, or counseled over the years, I find they often lack accountability in their lives, which thus leads to a lack of responsibility for the 168 hours in their week. They literally live haphazardly on a day-to-day basis. In particular, I posit that Y.A.G. will help reduce recidivism among adolescent males of color because of the disproportionate amount of adolescent males of color who experience high rates of juvenile incarceration (Horn, 2010; Kunjufu, 2005; Losen & Orfield, 2002; McGoldrick, Giordano, & Garcia-Preto, 2005; National Center for Health Statistics, 2010; Noguera, 2008; Richardson, 2008; Snyder & Sickmund, 2006).

Therefore, my rationale for Y.A.G. is to provide a safe space for incarcerated males of color to share among their peers an accountability process that will inevitably help them focus their time on preparing for and accomplishing professional and personal goals – reducing their recidivism rates within the JJC. The following describes the implementation processes of Y.A.G.

Y.A.G. Instructions

A. You are about to begin a process of holding people accountable for one another. You are not required to engage in this group. This group is optional. However, if you do wish to commit to the process, I ask that you pledge to at least one month of weekly attendance. If you agree to this one month commitment, please complete the attached goals, schedule, partner, and contract forms.

B. After you have decided to commit to Y.A.G. for one month and completed the paperwork for the assignment, beginning next month you will meet with your designated accountability partners in dyads during the group sessions. Moreover, it is very important to understand that committed participants must always have their goals/schedule present during every session. (See sample forms in Appendix A.)

Y.A.G. Purpose

The purpose of this accountability assignment is to engage incarcerated youth in holding each other accountable in an effort to achieve personal and professional goals while creating a supportive social network. Thus, it is important to understand that this activity is a fluid process, as you move through your life obtaining professional and personal goals.

Y.A.G. Assignment

In the attached "Youth Accountability Goals Form" (see Table A1 in Appendix A), write or type your name at the top of the form and then begin to (a) list all of your most current goals, (b) list the reason(s) for achieving each goal, (c) discuss the tasks and the statuses of each goal, and (d) insert a date of completion or explain your reason for terminating that goal. After you have completed filling out your goal form, please review your document for accuracy.

Y.A.G. Schedule

In the attached "Youth Accountability Schedule Form" (see Table A2 in Appendix A), write or type your name at the top of the form and then (a) list the exact activity that you are engaging in during each hour of the day, (b) insert your transitions throughout the day (e.g., eating, driving, etc.) by inserting the word "transition," and (c) review your documents for accuracy. For now, begin creating your documents by adding in times that say "at work," "studying for an exam," "with the kids," "with wife/husband at …." "With business partner(s)," "studying for school at library," " " "at the gym," "etc."

Practice creating names for your tasks and see if you can put in potential times with specifics. Only put actual activities inside the time slots when you are absolutely sure that you have that time slot allotted for a specific activity.

Y.A.G. Accountability Partner Form

The accountability partner form (see Table A3 in Appendix A) is a form that identifies members within the group whom you trust will hold you accountable on a monthly basis. More specifically, during each weekly check-in you should ask your accountability partner about the progression of goals or lack thereof. The dialogue process that occurs between accountability partners should be authentic and specific. For instance, a monthly dialogue can include a discussion of why some individuals are afraid of "achieving" their goals. Consequently, the topic regarding "fear of achievement" can be discussed comprehensively between accountability partners – specifically discussing the risks associated with achieving personal and professional goals.

Y.A.G. Monthly Contract Form

The monthly contract form (see Table A4 in Appendix A) is a way for everyone to write specific notes and sign after an extensive review of each other's goals and schedules. Every month, group leaders will provide specific feedback, along with group member's feedback, with a signature after group members have made specific comments. After specific comments are explained and understood, individuals will review and reflect upon suggested verbal and written feedback by group members and make the necessary adjustments to their Y.A.G. forms.

CHAPTER 10

CONCLUSION

Dr. Horn, I am sick of these White therapists....they don't know my boy...These White therapists are afraid to come to my house...He (the therapist) be droppin' my boy off at the corner after his appointment...This has got to stop Dr. Horn. We need therapists who are Black...who can relate to us...who understand my boy and his (explicative) issues that he be goin' through every day. (Parent Communication, Researcher Journal, 2010).

The above is a direct quote from one of my parents with whom I have worked for over four years. Her anger and frustrations about the lack of understanding and cultural awareness from her son's therapist are valid. I continue to hear similar frustrations from my parents regarding the lack of what I call the ability to relate with young Black males. I believe all caregivers, regardless of race, can improve their caregiving skills concerning young Black males.

Over the years I have reflected upon my practice with high-risk young Black males, especially my recent transition into becoming a therapist. What I found most influential was that I learned about my strengths as a therapist. Thus, my reflections have revealed five modalities that underserved youth and their families have complimented me on my use of each technique within their educational and mental health family counseling

The five modalities that have been most effective in my practice include: (1) my innate ability to care for and relate with young Black males, (2) my use of a structural family approach (see Boyd-Franklin, 2003), (3) my use of African-centered culture, (4) my inclusion of the extended Black family and (5) my use of the Black church. These modalities are explained in the following section.

Relating

For example, my ability to connect with Black males on a more profound level is by far my most significant strength. In addition, many of my clients inform me that I am extremely supportive and sensitive to their needs as a therapist. This reinforces my desire to persist in my academic training as a therapist.

As a therapist, I remain continually perplexed by the significance of how a therapeutic alliance (i.e., authentic trusting relationship) can positively impact therapy. Studies regarding therapeutic alliances have been found to enhance the treatment outcomes of severely depressed individuals, particularly those with dysthymic disorder (Castonguay et al., 2006). By this means, the therapeutic relationship developed between my clients and me allows us to delineate reasons for their current anxiety – absentee fathers, inadequate education, community violence, and poverty (Horn, 2010).

Most particularly, a structural family approach with high-risk young Black males may best serve their needs. Boyd-Franklin (2003) teaches that a structural family approach is a problem-solving approach to therapy that involves assessment of the family structure, identifying areas of difficulty, restructuring the family system in order to produce change, and creating clear treatment contracts. Likewise, Boyd-Franklin (2003) asserts that therapists working with adolescents who have been involved with violence need to be aware of the psychological impact of violence on adolescent Black males and their families.

Structural Family Approach

Boyd-Franklin (2003) reports "...very young children (as young as age 2) who have witnessed acts of violence have been diagnosed with posttraumatic stress disorder (PTSD) symptoms such as night terrors, repetitive play enactment of the experience, and flashbacks…" (p. 169). The author suggests repetitive play enactment and descriptive drawings as a specific technique that could be used to help discuss the trauma in therapy.

African-Centered Culture

In developing a tailored therapeutic plan for adolescent Black males who engage in violence, Wilson (1991) advises that counselors help adolescent Black males develop coping mechanisms such as immersing oneself in African-centered culture, establishing positive mentor relationships with African American males, and becoming involved in adolescent and anti-violent peer groups that focus on positive peer relations and communication skills.

Moreover, counselors and therapists can assist Black families by understanding the history of Black people, using the extended family in the therapeutic process, and understanding the impacts of racism and discrimination on the Black family (Bennett, 2005; McGoldrick et al., 2005). Furthermore, counselors must understand that although an increasing number of Black families are becoming single parent households, networks of extended family members aid in support (Hines & Boyd-Franklin, 2005; Sue & Sue, 2008).

The Extended Black Family

Sue and Sue (2008) discuss that "an extended family network…provides emotional and economic support….the rearing of children is often undertaken by a large number of relatives, older children, and close friends…" (p. 332). Hines and Boyd-Franklin (2005) also note that "A genogram can aid the therapist in gathering information about relationships and the roles of different family members" (p. 89). The extended family is key to understanding the complexity of the Black family structure. Counselors should consider the role of the extended family in each individual situation. These family members may be able to help co-facilitate a solution to a youth's involvement in violence.

The Black Church

As previously mentioned, the Black church has always played a pivotal role in the development of Black males. Counselors should realize that Black pastors can significantly influence the critical individuation and identity development processes in Black male development. Sue and Sue (2008) discuss the importance of churches by stating "A pastor or minister can help create sources of social support for family members....programs for the enrichment of family life may be developed jointly with the church..." (p. 336). Therefore, the Black church can help adolescent Black males to become individually responsible.

Although my book is not a one-size-fits-all for caregivers working with high-risk Black males, the primary intention is to improve relationships with young Black males by divulging impactful lifespan issues. For this reason, I have provided in this book prevalent issues that impact young Black males' lifespan development and resources to help assist caregivers. Hence, this book can be used to further advance research on improving relationships with young Black males. By understanding the broader issues that affect some young Black males, teachers, parents, advocates, professors, therapists, doctors, and lay people will be inspired to begin the journey of improving relationships with the young Black males to whom they provide caregiving services.

APPENDIX A

FORMS FOR YOUTH ACCOUNTABILITY GROUP

Table A1

Youth Accountability Group: Goals Form

					Professional Goals
Goal	**Reason(s)**	**Tasks**	**Status**	**Completion**	**Termination**

Table A2

Youth Accountability Group: Schedule Form

TIME	MON	TUE	WED	THU	FRI	SAT	SUN
4-5AM							
5-6AM							
6-7AM							
7-8AM							
8-9AM							
9-10AM							
[continues hourly]							
7-8PM							
8-9PM							
9-10PM							
10-11PM							
11-12AM							

TRANSITION:	1. TRAVEL	6. MEETINGS
(BLANK SPACES)	2. PHONE	7. PREPARATION
	3. FOOD	8. STUDY
	4. ERRANDS	9. FAMILY
	5. PAPERWORK	

Table A3

Youth Accountability Group: Accountability Partner Form

Name: _____	Name: _____
Phone: _____	Phone: _____
Address: _____	Address: _____
_____	_____
_____	_____
Email: _____	Email: _____
Name: _____	Name: _____
Phone: _____	Phone: _____
Address: _____	Address: _____
_____	_____
_____	_____
Email: _____	Email: _____

Table A4

Youth Accountability Group: Monthly Contract Form

I will pursue the following goals for the entire month from _____ to _____

GOALS:	
MONTHLY REVIEW:	My contract will be reviewed every week by a trusted friend or family member (i.e., accountability partner).
RECORD:	I completed _____ goals this week.
NOTES:	
MONTH OF:	
MY SIGNATURE:	
ACCOUNTABILITY PARTNER'S SIGNATURE:	

APPENDIX B

YOUTH ACCOUNTABILITY GROUP FLYER

Youth Accountability Group (Y.A.G.)

Come join us in a conversation about helping each other achieve our goals. All youth are invited to a weekly **Youth Accountability Group.** Please join the Staff as we help youth explore and achieve their goals while working with their peers in a safe environment.

APPENDIX C

SAMPLE EBONICS PHRASES

Table C1

Sample Ebonics Phrases Spoken by Adolescent Black Males in Urban Communities

PHRASE	MEANING
Bounce	To leave, go away, expeditiously
Beat Down or scraped on!	To get jumped and lose in a fight
Block	The street in which you live and represent
Blunt	Large marijuana cigarette usually rolled in cigar-type rolling paper
Chillin'	To Relax; to mind one's own business
Cool off dat	Not wanting to engage in a particular activity
Do me	Focusing solely on personal responsibilities
Do my thang	Focusing solely on personal responsibilities
Do your Thug thizal!	To be proud of someone taking care of their personal business
Elroy	Police
Fa real/ Fa sho	To be surprised or amazed
Get wit dem	To fight or interact with a group of people immediately
Holla	To engage in a discussion
Holla at chu boy	To inquire about someone's feeling; to communicate at a later date
Homie	Long-term committed friend.

Table C1 (continued)

Sample Ebonics Phrases Spoken by Adolescent Black Males in Urban Communities

PHRASE	MEANING
I got'cho back	To take care of a friend or love one with complete commitment
Jackin'	To commit robbery
Keep it on da real	Being truthful from a street perspective
Off da chain/ Off da hook	Referring to someone or something as crazy, out of control, bad
Po po	Police
Potna	To describe an unknown person
Scrap	To fight
Sweatin'	The feeling of being harassed by someone
That's family	Ascribing legitimacy to someone close
That's my boy	Ascribing legitimacy to someone close
That's peeps	Ascribing legitimacy to someone close
Trippin'	The act of acting strangely or being in a foul mood
What chu finna get into?	Interested about future activities
What up wit' him?	Asking someone about recent life events
Who Dat?	To inquire about the appearance of an unknown individual
You doin it like that!	To be surprised or amazed; To be proud of someone
You feel me	Inquiring understating or comprehension from someone
You off the cheesy	The act of being funny

REFERENCES

Ainsworth, M. D. S. (1967). *Infancy in Uganda: Infant care and the growth of love.* Baltimore, MD: John Hopkins University Press.

Ainsworth, M. D. S., Blehar, M., Walters, E., & Wall, S. (1978). *Patterns of attachment: A psychological study of the strange situation.* Mahwah, NJ: Lawrence Erlbaum Associates.

Ainsworth, M. D. S., & Witing, B. A. (1969). Attachment and exploratory behavior of one-year olds in a strange situation. In B. M. Foss (Ed.), *Determinants of infant behavior* IV. London: Methuen.

American Psychiatric Association. (2000). *Diagnostic and statistical manual of mental disorders* (4th ed.). Arlington, VA: Author.

Andreopoloulos, G.J. & Claude, R.P. (1997*). Human rights education for the twenty-first century.* Philadelphia, PA: University of Pennsylvania Press.

Arnett, J. (2000). A theory of development from the late teens through the twenties. *American Psychologist, 55,* 469-480.

Banks, J. A. (2005). Multicultural education: Characteristics and goals. In J. A. Banks, & C. A. M. Banks (Eds.). *Multicultural education: Issues and perspectives* (5th ed., pp. 3-30). Hoboken, NJ: John Wiley & Sons, Inc.

Bennett, L. (2003). *Before the Mayflower: A history of Black America* (6th ed.). Chicago, IL: Penguin Books.

Bowlby, J. (1969). *Attachment and loss, Vol. 1: Attachment.* New York, NY: Basic Books.

Boyd-Franklin, N. (1989). The multi-systems approach to the treatment of poor black families. In N. Boyd-Franklin, *Black families in therapy* (pp. 158-175). New York, NY: Guilford Press.

Boyd-Franklin, N. (2003). *Black Families in Therapy: Understanding the African American Experience* (2nd ed.). New York, NY: Guilford Press.

Brinson, M. (1998). Removing the mask roots of oppression through omission. In L. Delpit & T. Perry (Eds.), *The real Ebonics debate: Power, language, and the education of African American children* (pp. 134-135). Boston, MA: Beacon Press.

California Department of Education. (2008). *High school dropout rates*. Retrieved March 14, 2010, from http://www.cde.ca.gov/.

Carter, B., & McGoldrick, M. (1999). Overview: The expanded family life cycle. In B. Carter & M. McGoldrick (Eds.), *The expanded family life cycle: Individual, family and social perspectives* (3rd ed., pp. 1-26). Boston, MA: Allyn and Bacon.

Castonguay, L., Holtforth, M., Coombs, M.M., Bebernan, R., Kakouros, A., Boswell, J. Reid, J.J., & Jones, E.E. (2006). Relationship factors in treating dysphoric disorders. In L. Castonguay & L. Beutler (Eds.) *Principles of therapeutic change that work* (pp.65-81) New York, NY: Oxford University Press.

Coddle. (2002). In E. Jewell (Ed.), The Oxford desk dictionary and thesaurus (p. 144, 2nd ed.). New York, NY: Oxford University Press.

Coddle. (2005). The American heritage desk dictionary and thesaurus (p. 144). Boston, MA: Houghton Mifflin.

Dallard, S. (1990). *Ella Baker: A leader behind the scenes.* Englewood Cliffs, NJ: Silver Burdett Press.

Dance, J. (2009). *Tough fronts: The impact of street culture on schooling*. New York, NY: RoutledgeFalmer.

Daniels, L. (Producer), & Daniels, L. (Director). (2009). *Precious* [Motion picture]. United States: Lionsgate.

Delpit, L. (1995). *Other people's children*. New York, NY: The New Press.

Delpit, L., & Dowdy, J. K. (2002). *The skin that we speak*. New York, NY: The New Press.

Delpit, L. (1998). What should teachers do? Ebonics and culturally responsive instruction. In L. Delpit & T. Perry (Eds.), *The real Ebonics debate: Power, language, and the education of African American children* (pp. 17-25). Boston, MA: Beacon Press.

Delpit, L., & Perry, T. (Eds.). (1998). *The real Ebonics debate: Power, language, and the education of African American children*. Boston, MA: Beacon Press.

Dinkmeyer, D. (1996). *The parent's handbook. STEP*. Circle Pines, MN. American Guidance Service.

Duncan, G. (2005). Schooling as a moral enterprise: Rethinking educational justice fifty years after Brown. In D. Byrne, *Brown v. Board of Education: Its impact on public education* (pp. 195-212). Brooklyn, NY: The Thurgood Marshall Scholarship Fund.

Epstein, N., Ryan, C., Bishop, D., Miller, I., & Keitner, G. (2003). The McMaster model: A view of healthy family functioning. In F. Walsh (Ed.), *Normal family processes* (3rd ed., pp. 581-607). New York: Guilford Press.

Erikson, E. H., & Erikson, J. M. (1998). The life cycle completed. New York, NY: W.W. Norton & Company, Inc.

Ewing, H., Grady, R. (Directors). (2005). *The boys of Baraka* [Film]. (Available from THINKFilm, 155 Avenue of the Americas, 7th Floor, NY, NY 10013)

Gordon, E. (2006). Establishing a system of public education in which all children achieve at high levels and reach their full potential. In T. Smiley, *The covenant with Black America.* (pp. 23-45). Chicago, IL: The World Press.

Himelstein, S. (2011). Transpersonal psychotherapy with incarcerated adolescents. *The Journal of Transpersonal Psychology*, *43*(1), 35-49. Retrieved from http://www.atpweb.org/

Hines, P., Boyd-Franklin, N. (2005). African American families. In M. McGoldrick, J. Giordano, & N. Garcia-Preto (Eds.), *Ethnicity & family therapy* (pp. 87-100). New York, NY: The Guilford Press.

Hoover, M. (1998). Ebonics speakers and cultural, linguistic, and political test bias. In L. Delpit & T. Perry (Eds.), *The real Ebonics debate: Power, language, and the education of African American children* (pp. 126-133). Boston, MA: Beacon Press.

Horn, A. (2010). *The role of father-like care in the education of young Black males.* New York, NY: Edwin Mellen Press.

Identity. (2007). APA dictionary of psychology (p. 463). Washington, DC: American Psychological Association.

Insaba, D., & Cohen, W. (2007). *Uppers, downers, all arounders. Physical and mental effects of psychoactive drugs.* Medford, OR: CNS Publications, Inc.

Kunjufu, J. (2005). *Keeping Black boys out of special education.* Chicago, IL: African American Images.

Ladson-Billings, G. (2004). Landing on the wrong note: The price we paid for *Brown*. *Educational Researcher*, *33*, 3-13.

Ladson-Billings, G. & Tate, W. F. (1995). Toward a critical race theory of education. *Teachers College Record, 97*(1), 47-69.

Lawrence, E. C. (1998). The humanistic approach of Virginia Satir. In D. Lawson & F. Prevatt (Eds.) *Casebook in family therapy* (pp. 169-187). Belmont, CA: Brooks/Cole

Lee, S. (Director). (1992). *Malcolm X* [Film]. (Available from Warner Brothers, 5800 Sunset Boulevard, Hollywood, CA 91505)

Lenahart, S. (2001). *Sociocultural and historical contexts of African American English.* Philadelphia, PA: John Benjamins Publishing Company.

Lewis, T., Amini, F., & Lannon, R. (2000). *A general theory of love.* New York, NY: Random House Inc.

Levin, F., McDowell, D., Evans, S. M., Nunes, E., Akerele, E., Donovan, S., & Vosburg, S. K. (2004). Pharmacotherapy for marijuana dependence: A double-blind, placebo-controlled pilot study of divalproex sodium. *The American Journal on Addictions, 13*(1), 21-32. doi:10.1080/10550490490265280

Litt, M. D., Kadden, R. M., Kabela-Cormier, E., & Petry, N. M. (2008). Coping skills training and contingency management treatments for marijuana dependence: Exploring mechanisms of behavior change. *Addiction, 103*(4), 638-648. doi:10.1111/j.1360-0443.2008.02137.x

Losen, D., & Orfield, G. (2002). *Racial inequality in special education.* Cambridge, MA: Harvard University Press.

Martin, W. E. (1998). *Brown v. Board of Education should have said. A brief history with documents.* New York, NY: Bedford/ St. Martin's.

McGoldrick, M., Giordano, J., & Garcia-Preto, N. (2005). *Ethnicity & family therapy.* New York, NY: The Guilford Press.

Means-Coleman, R. R. & Daniel, J. L. (2000). Mediating Ebonics. *Journal of Black Studies, 31,* 74-95. Retrieved on November 2, 2005 from http://0-web26.epnet.com.ignacio.usfca.edu

Meier, T. (1998). Teaching teachers about Black communications. In L. Delpit & T. Perry (Eds.), *The real Ebonics debate: Power, language, and the education of African American children* (pp. 117-125). Boston, MA: Beacon Press.

Mendez et al. v. Westminster School District of Orange County et al., 64F. (Supp., 1946) U.S. Dist. LEXIS 2789 (S.S. California 1946). Retrieved May 21, 2007, from Lexis Nexis.

Merriweather-Moore, L. (2004). *Voices of successful African American men.* New York, NY: The Edwin Mellen Press.

National Center for Health Statistics. (2010). *Estimates of the July 1, 2000-July 1, 2009, United States resident population from the Vintage 2009 postcensal series by year, county, age, sex, race, and Hispanic origin.* Retrieved from http://www.ojjdp.gov/ojstatbb/ezapop/asp/profile_selection.asp

Nichols, M. (2010). *Family therapy. Concepts and methods.* Boston, MA: Allyn & Bacon.

Noguera, P. (2008). The trouble with Black boys. And other reflections on race, equity, and the future of public education. San Francisco, CA: Jossey-Bass.

O'Neil, W. (1998). If Ebonics isn't a language, then tell me, what is? In L. Delpit & T. Perry (Eds.), *The real Ebonics debate: Power, language, and the education of African American children* (pp. 38-47). Boston, MA: Beacon Press.

Perry, T. (1998). "I'on know why they be trippin'": Reflections on the Ebonics debate. In L. Delpit & T. Perry (Eds.), *The real Ebonics debate: Power, language, and the education of African American children* (pp. 3-15). Boston, MA: Beacon Press.

Phelan, T. (2003). *1-2-3. Magic: effective discipline for children 2-12.* Glen Ellyn, IL: Parent Magic, Inc.

Richardson, J. B. Jr., (2008). Contextualizing juvenile re-entry for young African American males: From prison yard to schoolyard. *Journal of Public Management & Social Policy, 14,* 21-32. Retrieved from https://sites.google.com/a/jpmsp.com/www/volume14issue

San Francisco NAACP v. San Francisco Unified School District, 413 F. (Supp., 2005) U.S. Dist. LEXIS 30189 (S.S. California 2005). Retrieved April 22, 2007, from Lexis Nexis.

Santrock, J. (2009). *Life-span development.* New York, NY: McGraw-Hill.

Schott Foundation for Public Education. (2008). Public education and black male students. Retrieved March 13, 2010, from http://schottfoundation.org/.

Seligman, M. E. P., Rashid, T., & Parks, A. C. (2006). Positive psychotherapy. *American Psychologist, 61*(8), 774-788.

Siegel, D., & Hartzell, M. (2003). *Parenting from the inside out.* New York, NY: Tarcher/Penguin.

Sinha, R., Easton, C., Renee-Aubin, L., & Carroll, K. M. (2003). Engaging young probation-referred marijuana-abusing individuals in treatment: A pilot trial. *The American Journal on Addictions, 12*(4), 314-323. doi:10.1080/10550490390226905

Smiley, T. (2006). *The covenant in action.* Los Angeles, CA: The Smiley Group, Inc.

Smiley, T. (2006). *The covenant with Black America.* Chicago, IL: The World Press.

Smith, E. (1998). What is Black English? What is Ebonics? In L. Delpit & T. Perry (Eds.), *The real Ebonics debate: Power, language, and the education of African American children* (pp. 49-58). Boston, MA: Beacon Press.

Smitherman, G. (1998). Black English/Ebonics: What it be like? In L. Delpit & T. Perry (Eds.), *The real Ebonics debate: Power, language, and the education of African American children* (pp. 29-37). Boston, MA: Beacon Press.

Smitherman, G. (1998). "What go round come round": King in perspective. In L. Delpit & T. Perry (Eds.), *The real Ebonics debate: Power, language, and the education of African American children* (pp. 163-171). Boston, MA: Beacon Press.

Suarez-Orozco, M. (2004). Formulating identity in a globalized world. In M. Suarez-Orozco & D. Qin-Hilliard (Eds.), *Globalization. culture and education in the new millennium.* (pp. 173-201). Boston, MA: Beacon Press.

Synder, H., & Sickmund, M. (2006). *Juvenile offenders and victims: 2006 national report.* Washington, DC: U.S. Department of Justice, Office of Justice Programs, Office of Juvenile Justice and Delinquency Prevention. Retrieved from http://www.ojjdp.gov/ojstatbb/nr2006/downloads/chapter3.pdf

Sue, D. W., & Sue, D. (2008). *Counseling the culturally diverse. Theory and practice.* Hoboken, NJ: Wiley & Sons, Inc.

Vetere, A. (2001). Structural family therapy. *Child Psychology & Psychiatry Review, 6*(3), 133-139. DOI: 10.1017/S1360641701002672

Weissbrodt, D., Fitzpatrick, J., Newman, F., Hoffman, M. & Rumsey, M. (2001). *Selected international human rights instruments and bibliography for research on human rights law.* (3rd ed.) Cincinnati, OH: Anderson Publishing Company.

White, M., & Epston, D. (1990). *Narrative means to therapeutic ends.* New York, NY: W.W. Norton.

White, J., & Cones, J. (1999). *Black man emerging. Facing the past and seizing a future in America.* New York, NY: W.H. Freeman and Company.

Wilcox, R. (1971). *The psychological consequences of being a Black American. A sourcebook of research by Black psychologists.* New York, NY: John Wiley & Sons, Inc.

Wilson, A. (1991). *Understanding Black adolescent male violence. Its remediation and prevention.* New York, NY: Afrikan World Infosystems.

INDEX

AFTERWORD

In the past, I have not been given the writing space to thank those who have supported me throughout my lifespan development as a Black male – the people who "Got my Back!" Therefore, in this section of my book I will now take the time to thank those who have allowed me to grow and develop into the Black man I am today. In my first book, ***The Role of Father-like Care in the Education of Young Black Males***, I plea with my readers to urge our public schools to increase the number of Black male mentors. Although this plea may have gone unheard, I fight every day to develop a task force of professionals who can assist my efforts to help young Black males.

Over the past twenty years, I have worked arduously to train Black men who can serve as mentors, teachers, and counselors for young Black males from underserved communities, particularly those in the public school system. I soon came to realize that recruiting Black men in the city of San Francisco and the greater Bay Area was unrealistic for various reasons. Some of these reasons include a Black exodus, high incarceration rates, institutionalized racism, and other factors similar to the issues that impact the lifespan development of young Black males.

Thus, I have come to the understanding that in order to serve the thousands of young Black males who live in the most deprived neighborhoods of San Francisco and the greater Bay Area, I need the help of all mentors, teachers, and counselors; regardless of race and ethnicity, gender, socioeconomic status, sexuality, ablebodiness, etc. Therefore, the following are individuals who I consider my extended family. These individuals have supported me throughout my career. They include a host of family member's friends, and colleagues who represent the essence of "I Got'Cho Back!" I would like to personally extend my gratitude to all of the following extended family members who have helped me, in various ways, assist the thousands of young

Black males that I have worked with over the past twenty years of my professional career.

First and foremost, to Dr. Ben Baab, like my favorite rapper Jay Z says, "What more can I say!" You are amazing! What a true mentor you have been over the years – you are caring, consistent, and honest! Your editing has allowed me to publish two books and counting!

Secondly, I would like to thank Ms. Deborah Gerosa for taking her valuable time, spirituality, energy, and resources to create such a magnificent book cover. Your paintings are an inspiration to the human soul! God Bless you Deborah!

To Mr. Dave Scott and family, thank you for your committed friendship to my family for over thirty years. You have been a role model for thousands of young Black males. Most important, your mentorship has allowed me to become an effective teacher and future therapist.

To the Steeno Family (Jeff, Connie, Axel, and Chuy), thank you for inspiring me to become Dr. Horn. You have been my extended family for over ten years. Your love, genuineness, and hospitality have blessed my professional and personal growth beyond words.

To Dr. Lois Merriweather-Moore, words cannot explain how much your mentorship has meant to me over the past seven years. You poured into me your spirit of writing and I have ascended since then! Thank you for imparting your gift of writing into my soul!

To Cousin Chris, thank you for always "having my back" while growing up! You always took care of me when we hung out. I will never forget our friendship, which extended beyond family, as we graduated from college together. I love you cuzzo!

To Auntie Jeannie and Cousin Demetrius, thank you for supporting all of my academic and personal dreams. Auntie Jeannie, I appreciate the way you raised me while growing up and I will never forget your gift of caregiving that you used to raise my brother and me.

To Cousin Demetrius, thank you for being a young man of God and watching out for my Auntie Jeannie. Out of all the gifts I admire in you, I appreciate you taking care of my auntie the most. I am so proud of your positive development since your childhood.

To Uncle Lucias, thank you for teaching and encouraging me through godliness! You always had a kind word to say that included a message from the Bible. I am thankful for you because your biblical teaching helped me stay encouraged all throughout college.

To Cousin Donnell, thank you for teaching me about the streets! As a young child, you persistently infused your knowledge about the streets within my lifespan development. I will always remember the most important skills that no school could have ever taught me – street life!

To Cousin Janetta, thank you for always checking in with me. I enjoy our conversations on the nuances of gender issues, especially from a strong Black woman's perspective. Most of all, I highly value your willingness to converse in depth regarding male/female relationships.

To Cousin Chris Horn, thank you for always being there for me throughout my lifespan development. You have always kept in touch with my family over the years regardless of my whereabouts. I will continually remember your commitment to family closeness.

To Dr. Farbod Karimi and family, thank you for being an incredible blessing in my life. Your friendship over the past seven years has taught me how to become a caring professional while maintaining a sense of humor. Thank you for modeling these skills in our friendship!

To my dear friend and her partner (Soma and Waldemar), thank you Soma for keeping your word and staying connected with my family. You remain a special part of my life. Your true friendship with my family is a sign of your authenticity as a human being.

To my dear fraternity brothers of Alpha Phi Alpha (Xi Rho Chapter), thank you for your passion to educate and uplift the Black community, especially young Black males. I am so proud to belong to a brotherhood of strong Black men who unceasingly serves the Black community.

In particular, I would like to thank my fraternity brother Mr. Larry Goode for your dependable friendship. Larry, your unshakable friendship has demonstrated that Black men need and benefit from life-long mentorship. You represent the heart of I Got'Cho Back!

To Sean Clinton, thank you for modeling the professionalism of an Alpha Phi Alpha man. You have always been uplifting and spiritual. Your service to the youth of the Bay Area is incomparable to that of anyone I know. I am proud to be your fraternity brother!

To my best friend Maurice Lewis, thank you for being another true accountability partner. Our friendship spans over two decades. Your commitment and dedication to the Black community as a Special Education teacher inspires me to continue my work every day!

To my best friend, Mr. Robert Lucas and Family (Alana, Brian and David), thank you Rob Luke for being the best accountability partner ever. Your profound advice has significantly impacted my personal and professional development.

To my best friend and Fraternity brother (AQA) Reggie Stewart and family (Lee, Nia, and Noa), thank you for always treating me as "Uncle Aaron!" Watching you guys (Reggie and Lee) become doctors of education while raising my niece and nephew has motivated me to become a better human being.

To my best friend, Mr. Johnny Sellers, thank you Johnny for being a dependable friend over the past twenty years. Our friendship is a demonstration of how true friendships can last the course of a lifespan while living in two different geographical regions of the United States.

To my Big Brother and Fraternity brother (AQA) Calvin, thank you for supporting my research from day one. You are the role model for "Father-like Care," especially with your son Darius. I look forward to working with you in the future!

To my best friend of twenty plus years, Delmar Johnson and family (Tracy and Jeaneen). Delmar, thank you for being a true friend. Over the past twenty years we have seen our shares of ups and downs but we are still here together! Thank you Big D for being a loyal friend!

To my homies, Brad and Onllwyn (Dr. Washington and Dr. Dixon), having you two strong Black men in my life has increased my courage as a professional Black male. Thank you for navigating America with me while maintaining our legacy, self-confidence, and Black pride.

To the Sheppard Family (Edward, Neashelle, and Tiye), thank you for all of your support and for giving birth to my magnificent niece, Ms. Tiye Sheppard. I am still overwhelmed at what a fabulous young lady you have raised – entering college at age 16.

Tiye, your commitment to our weekly check-ins over the past two years have been remarkable. In addition, your passion for educating people of color and for being such a dedicated college student has made me a very proud uncle! Continue your road to greatness!

To my dear brother and sister-in-law, Kenny and Christina, thank you for supporting your brother through yet another degree and book. Your love and commitment towards one another has been wonderful to watch over the years.

To Kenny, thank you for always supporting my work. You alone were the first to purchase my book and you alone continue to be the largest supplier of my first book. That speaks volumes about your true friendship.

To my new friend and accountability partner (Mr. Cecil Wong and family), thank you Cecil for your continuous prayers and friendship. I am looking forward to years of fellowship and worship together as friends of the same faith. I genuinely appreciate your conviction to God!

To my sister and her family (Karla, Alex, and Sebastian), thank you Karla for keeping me in your prayers and thoughts over the years. It's a blessing to have you in my life as my familia, especially watching my little nephew Sebastian grow up so fast! God Bless you!

To my sister Guilaine and her family, thank you Guilaine for our faithful decade of friendship. Our friendship proves that the friendships we establish throughout our careers can extend beyond the places we meet. Thank you for modeling the meaning of extended family!

To Belinda Arriaga, words cannot explain how you have impacted my life. You have always been by my side – another true accountability partner. Your encouragement, wisdom, positive energy, and straightforward advice have blessed me infinitely.

To my sister Andrea McEvoy-Spero and Family (Jason, Ella, and Maya). Andrea, you have truly been an amazing sister who walks the talk of a passionate and caring educator. I am truly blessed to be your surrogate Big Brother!

To the Psyhogios family (Suzette, Tim, and Ross), thank you for showing me what caring family members do for one another. Your love as a mother Suzette for your son has exemplified the necessity and impact of a mother's unrelenting love for her child.

Ross, thank you for being such a committed passionate young brother. Regardless of your personal struggles you have endured, you have successfully completed undergraduate and law school at a very young age – well ahead of your peer group. I am so proud of you!

To the Griffin family (Byron, Susan, Jeron, and Aislynn), thank you for your continual steadfast friendship since our army days as Airborne Rangers! Byron, you continue to model the true role model of a man of God! I will never forget the way you prayed with me in the army!

I would like to extend a special thank you to all of the Black professors and staff (Dr. Moore, Dr. Taylor, Dr. Dixon, Dr. Washington, Dr. Cannon, Dr. Mitchell, and others) who stand up for the students of color at the University of San Francisco, I graciously thank you!

To Dr. Tyrone Cannon and my USF Gleeson library family (Carmen, Joe, Collette, Matt, Lloyd, Shawn, Sherise, Fabiola, etc.), thank you for allowing me to keep my office space in the library for the past seven years as a doctorate and masters student.

To Tyrone, thank you for your counsel, check-ins, and humor - they have immeasurably enriched my soul. You have been a true mentor by just listening and laughing with me. Your mentorship has modeled the type of mentor I would like to be for other Black males in the future.

To Joe Garity, thank you for your continuous support for my research. You continue to be a steadfast friend and mentor, particularly with assisting my research with impoverished families of color. I genuinely appreciate your true friendship.

To Collette, thank you for always encouraging my writing effort over the seven years I have been a member of the Gleeson Library family. Your encouragement has prompted me to establish an overpowering morning ritual of writing.

To Sherise, thank you for engaging in thoughtful discussions about matters that impact people of color over the past five years in passing. I will always value your excitement to converse about cultural issues. You are a valiant librarian woman of color.

To Fabiola, thank you for engaging in conversations about culture over the past five years. I always appreciate our honest dialogues about underserved communities. More important, I am so proud that you have gone back to school to obtain your MS in library science.

To Ms. Kathleen Elizabeth Quinn, thank you for sharing your passion of travel with me. I will never forget our honest conversations about traveling abroad. Your passion for travel inspires me to see the entire world!

To Dr. Suzan Katz, thank you for always believing in my ability to lead youth. Your belief in me has inspired me to become a life-long teacher, counselor, and caregiver for males of color, especially young Black males.

To Donna Sellers and my USF Counseling Psychology family (Estella, Dr. Bussolari, Dr. Peltier, Dr. Flores, Dr. Coombs, Dr. Adams, Dr. Goodell, Professor Linda Klann, Professor Sam Garanzini, Dr. Terence Patterson, and others), thank you for keeping me motivated throughout the entire program.

To Donna, I was always taught that the most important person in any organization is the administrative assistant. You symbolize that lesson in so many ways. Thank you for always affectionately greeting every person who comes through your door every day.

To Estella Pabonan, thank you for our monthly check-ins. You have been an incredible friend by helping me navigate the field of counseling, especially the incredible amounts of paperwork. Your administrative skills are unparalleled!

To Dr. Cori Bussolari, thank you for always allowing me the safe space in your office to share my passion of counseling males of color. You have always allowed time for me to discuss my life and I will never forget your willingness to share your time.

To Dr. Elena Flores, thank you for giving me the courage to start the first Student of Color Support Group at the University of San Francisco, Counseling Psychology program. Your mentorship and counseling buffered the microaggressions I encountered as a Black male.

To Dr. Judy Goodell, thank you for teaching me about the lifespan development of human beings. I learned some of the most valuable therapeutic tools that I will never forget. Because of you alone, I am now in therapy with a Black male therapist whom I adore!

To Dr. Mary Coombs, thank you for being a true mentor and counselor. Your guidance and validation of my work continues to drive my passion for working with underserved families of color. I am grateful to have you in my life as my mentor.

To Dr. Maureen Adams, thank you for always demonstrating the power of the therapeutic group. I learned from your class that group therapy can be truly inspirational when the therapist can strategically create a space that is both comfortable and safe for group participants.

To Dr. Bruce Peltier, thank you for always being real and transparent! From the moment we met, you have been nothing but an honest person who holds himself and others accountable – you have modeled to me and others what it's like to be a man of integrity!

To Professor Linda Klann, thank you for teaching me effective parenting techniques from Dinkmeyer's (1996) STEP program. I appreciate your inspiration for improving parent-child relationships!

To Professor Sam Garanzini, thank you for teaching me about drug and alcohol abuse, especially the negative impacts on the brain. Because of your data, I successfully educate my clients (predominantly young Black males) on the negative effects of marijuana.

To Dr. Terence Patterson, thank you for demonstrating your passion for ethics with the MFT students. I have learned some invaluable lessons from your teaching. Most significant, I learned to constantly refer to my MFT Code of Ethics manual as a standard of therapeutic practice.

To all of my USF MFT graduate classmates (Beth, Liberty, Selma, Tula, Lesley, Rian, Maddie, Eddie, Bernie Mac, Jazzy, Victoria (Tori), Alisa, Jackie, Dave, Joe, Cassidy, Christine, Aloralyn, Vanessa, John and others), thank you for supporting my career transition from educator to therapist.

To Aloralyn, thank you for always being a phenomenal listener and friend. You consistently model someone who is present and attentive. I value your transparency as a person and your candidness.

To my sister from another mother, Beth Lee, thank you for always allowing me to be a part of your family, including your sons, sisters, and your husband (my brother-in-law) Marcus. Our monthly check-ins has been a true sanctification to my soul!

To my Hermana, Liberty Velez, what a true sister. Your prayers, friendship, and unconditional love have impacted me for a lifetime. Thank you for allowing me to be a part of your family. Your honesty is what I admire the most about you.

To my sister and brother-in-law, Selma Schlesinger and Matt, thank you for always welcoming me into your home. You have been a tremendous blessing to me because of the love you illustrate to me, your consistent friendship, and your authentic hospitality.

To my sister Lesley Guth! Thank you for demonstrating that friendship can endure the test of times. Your steadfast friendship is a true testament to the power of authentic, genuine, relationships – I can see why the kids you work with trust you with their life!

To my sister Tula, thank you for being a true friend and confidant. When I was struggling personally, you never missed a beat. You have been by my side from the beginning of the program until now. I truly respect your unwavering friendship!

To my sister and brother-in-law, Rian and John, thank you Rian for being an incredible sister to me through the program. Our friendship has endured some personal trials and tribulations. Thank you for loving your brother through the good and bad times.

To Madeleine Mandich, thank you for being such an inspiration in my life. Your love for counseling students has encouraged me to continue the work that I do every day. Your inspiration, especially that smile, has been a blessing to me!

To my friend and accountability partner Eddie Grassi, thank you for always being real and vulnerable about your life. Our friendship has taught me that men can establish true authentic relationships, especially when it comes to actively listening to one another.

To Dave Nogradi, thank you for always being another true accountability partner. Our shared passion and commitment for accountability has allowed our friendship to grow beyond the classroom. I appreciate your true friendship.

To Christine, thank you for always checking in with me throughout the MFT program. Your attunement to me during the program allowed me to navigate racial microaggressions and complete the MFT program. I will always value your ability to motivate people!

To Tori, my other sister, thank you for being an advocate, teacher, and future therapist for underserved families, particularly young Black males. I will never forget the way you cared for the young boys in your trainceship. You epitomize the role of caregiver as a teacher!

To Alisa, thank you for being the kindest little sister in the world. Your smile and commitment to children with autism will never be forgotten. It was a blessing to have worked with you on our various research projects and class presentations.

To Cassidy Marie Miller and family, thank you Cassidy for sharing your gift of patience, reflection, and calmness with me. Because of your friendship, you allowed me to make more time for God and self-reflection in my life. Thank you for rekindling my relationship with God!

To Vanessa, thank you for always being the most responsive classmate I have ever known. I will always remember you for your kindness and quiet activism for students of color. I appreciate your authentic care and love for your community, family and friends.

To my counseling family (Ebony, Karen, and Aaqilah), thank you for supporting my passion for counseling underserved families of color. All three of you have been a tremendous inspiration to my personal and professional development. I sincerely thank you for your advice!

To Karen, you epitomize the Rogerian belief that human beings can reach their fullest potential under the mutual trust and care in a relationship! Thank you for demonstrating a reciprocal trusting relationship with me. You are an outstanding mentor!

To Ebony, you represent the true womanhood of Black femininity – strong, resilient, and relentless! When I see you, I see the reflection of the Black community in your soul. Thank you Ebony for holding me accountable to myself and the Black community!

To Aaqilah, you are a woman of valor and principle. I will always cherish your passion to serve the Black community and other underserved communities of color with such conviction and passion. Thank you for modeling transparency as a therapist!

To all of my mentees (Kagiso, Lawrence, Eric, Sue, Stephanie, Chris Lee, and others), thank you for always being inspirational and motivated! All of you have been a pleasure to mentor over the past several years. I look forward to mentoring you for years to come!

To my little brother Kagiso Molefe, thank you for your persistent friendship over the past several years. I enjoy mentoring you as my little brother because you continue to set the bar high for yourself and other young Black males around you.

To Lawrence, I am so proud of you. You repeatedly set goals for yourself to accomplish every year. I look forward to mentoring you for years to come. You have become a man of accountability and self-determination.

To Eric Taylor, I definitely Got' Cho Back! Although you and I exist among a hand full of soon-to-be Black male therapists, we have stood by each other's side. I will continue to mentor you as long as humanly possible! I Got' Cho Back!

To Sue Sullivan, thank you for being such a magnificent accountability partner. Your candidness and humor have allowed me to grow professionally and personally. I appreciate your commitment to genuine relationship and accountability.

To Stephanie Willis, thank you for being a faithful accountability partner. Your pure heart and truthfulness to our relationship has allowed me to believe that they are relationships that exist that are non-transactional.

To Chris Lee, I am so proud of your growth over the past five years that we have known each other. You have grown into a young man who is accountable, reliable, and passionate about people with disabilities. I appreciate your passion to serve the mental health community.

To my Koret Health and Recreation Center family (Chuck, Todd, Dre, Brian, and others), thank you for providing such a wonderful gym for me to release my stress during the week.

To Todd, you are a magnificent trainer and role model who is truly accountable to himself and his community! Thank you for allowing me the space to talk candidly about our vision for the Black community.

To all of my clients and their families, I am greatly appreciative of your prayers, support, and reassurance. Because of you, I am able to exist within this field as a passionate advocate for underserved families.

A special thanks to Mr. Stefan Jackson for supporting my writing efforts throughout the years as I graciously walked in and out of FedEx Kinko's printing and scanning documents. Thank you for your continual encouragement regarding my work with young Black males.

To Shawn Harris, thank you for always supporting my professional endeavors each time we talked at the FedEx Kinko's office. Your encouragement has allowed me to endure the demanding professional market that exists within San Francisco! I appreciate your counsel!

To all of the dynamic Black male teachers, mentors, and counselors (especially Mr. Claudius Johnson) in the San Francisco Bay

Area, thank you for always being there for us Black males. We need you and value your support and service to our community.

To Mr. Neal Hatten, thank you for teaching me about community advocacy. I will never forget the leadership skills that I observed in you twenty years ago as I worked under your mentorship. You showed me how to serve my community with the utmost care and humility.

To Micheal Bennett, thank you for serving the community of Bayview Hunter's Point. Your service to this community, which is near and dear to my heart, has been a tremendous blessing to the citizens of Bayview and other surrounding communities.

To Shakeel Ali, thank you for encouraging me through your commitment to anti-bullying. You are a beacon of change for the Bay Area regarding violence prevention and community safety. I applaud your community advocacy and dedication to community safety.

To Nathan Cleveland, thank you for being a role model for young Black men in the military and in the civilian community. It has been a blessing to mentor you and watch you grow into an honorable young man with strong values.

To Trent, thank you for being a man of integrity! Throughout the years we have engaged in critically conscious raising dialogues each and every time I come into Sears Automotive. I value our friendship and look forward to our impending discussions in the near future.

To Ms. Rebecca Fall, I have never witnessed a teacher with so much patience and love for children with special needs. I truly appreciate your service to the Black community for working so tolerantly with our young Black males in special education.

To Mr. Paul Oglesby, thank you for sharing your therapeutic gift with the young Black males and their families you have provided therapy to over your professional career. I appreciate your effort and belief in the value of community mental health.

I must extend a very exceptional thank you to Dr. Saralyn Ruff for introducing me to the topic of Intersectionality. Because of your mentorship, I have now launched my career as a therapist intern into new unchartered territories within the field of community mental health.

To my good friend and mentor for over ten years, Mr. Paul Harris. Thank you for maintaining our friendship beyond the United States military. I will always admire your persistent commitment to soldiers, especially your ability to mentor soldiers and civilians.

To Mr. Paul Robertson, thank you for serving underserved communities for over thirty years. You personify the ideal community advocate because of your demonstrated mentoring, teaching, and counseling of K-12 youth. I am thankful for our thirty years of friendship!

To Mr. Lee Hightower, I am so proud of your accomplishments! You are a young Black man who has risen to the top of his game! Thank you for inspiring the young Black males in my practice to continue with their dreams of pursuing graduate studies in Ivy League schools.

To Ms. Pepper Black, thank you for demonstrating your passion for domestic violence prevention. Your ability to enhance communication efforts among couples and provide safety for domestic violence victims has significantly improved my professional development.

To Helen Huynh, thank you for being my new accountability partner. Since we met, you have participated in personal accountability dialogues that have demonstrated truthfulness and commitment to personal improvement. I appreciate your honest friendship.

To Auntie Elizabeth and Uncle Barney, thank you for opening up your land to me while I visited the beautiful sanctuary of the Big Island. Your home removed my anxiety and stress of the mainland during the first day of my arrival. Thank you for your hospitality!

To Gianni, Devon and Angela, thank you for creating a safe space for me to be myself while visiting your restaurant. I have truly been blessed by the conversations, personal stories, and laughter we all shared when I visited the Big Island. Thank you for making me feel at home!

To Mr. Christian Lindner and Ms. Sasha Monteiro, thank you for being my European voices of reason. I appreciate the time we spent together over the summer and will never forget our candid dialogues concerning our shared passion for educating young children.

To Mr. Mehrshad Yazdi, thank you for being my new accountability partner. I appreciate your enthusiasm to meet with me monthly to discuss personal issues and shared passions. I look forward to meeting with you in the future to connect on a more profound level.

To all of my uncles and cousins on the Horn and Jackson side of the family, I give you a special thank you! To all of you, including Auntie Betty, Uncle Larry, Cousin Lawrence, Cousin Jazmine, Cousin Marlena, Cousin Etecia, Cousin Nailah, Saffron, Cousin Shawn, Cousin Shawnisha, Cousin Elaina, Cousin Tierra, Uncle Lionel, Cousin Pierre, Uncle Tony, Cousin Miki, Cousin Michelle, Cousin Russell, Uncle Tony, Cousin Anthony, Uncle Lionel, Cousin Naomi, Cousin Nikki, Uncle Roland, Auntie Reggie, Cousin Chris, Cousin Suzy, Uncle Austin, Uncle Wayne, and Uncle Michael. Thank you for always keeping the family together through family outings, barbeques and celebrations.

Auntie Betty (aka momma Boo), thank you for praying for me my entire life, especially with my momma when I was stationed in the military. As the Bible says, "the prayers of the righteous availeth much…" you epitomize the true Christian spirit by acting with prayer. I love you auntie!

Cousin Marlena, I want to thank you personally for being a tremendous blessing in my life! You are my spiritual guide! Thank you for always believing in me and trusting me to help support your dreams and endeavors with your phenomenal organization -

Nexgenegirls! I look forward to enjoying our combined process of professional development as we travel down the road to professional success and achievement as cousins!

To the strong Black male barbers who have been significant in my growth as an educated and articulate Black man, I would like to thank Pete and Dynamite. As I always like to discuss with my colleagues, the sacred conversations that have taken place in your barbershop when I was growing up have inspired me infinitely. Thank you for enhancing my critical consciousness and for challenging me to think outside of the box. I appreciate you and respect you both as the foundational leaders of the Bay View Hunters Point Community.

To my business consultant and Fraternity Brother (AQA) Mr. Mauricio Wright, thank you for keeping me honest by holding me accountable for my clients and students and for pushing me to improve my skill sets and challenging me to go beyond my comfort zone professionally. You are a Godsend!

To my nutritionist, Mr. Gary Yee, thank you for seeping your valuable time to work with me one-on-one over the past year. Your counsel on nutrition and diet have helped me lose weight and sustain a manageable weight as I navigate my middle adulthood.

To the 3rd Street Youth Center and Clinic (Ayanna, Aliya, Darrell, Katie, Joi, Winnie, and Ronnishia) thank you for allowing me the opportunity to continue using my gift of counseling with underserved youth and families. I give a special thanks to Mr. Michael Baxter and Mrs. Maureen McCarthy for hiring me as a volunteer.

Most significant, to Ms. Ronnishia Johnson, thank you for being there for me since the start of my internship – day one! You have been the "spark" in my professional career. In our short time together as colleagues, you demonstrate to me on a daily basis that nonprofits can still be productive forces in the lives of underserved families. You are an inspiration to all young Delta Sigma Theta women across the country.

To Joi Jackson, thank you for being my prayer partner and angel in disguise. Your prayers for my salvation, protection and encouragement have guided me through this process of being one of only a few Black male mental health interns. Thank you for always having my back like a true sista through prayer.

To all of my colleagues at the Balboa Teen health Center; Mrs. Maureen McCarthy, Mr. Michael Baxter, Ms. Agnes Wong, Mrs. Hillary Walsh, Mrs. Kim Tucker, Ms. Liliana Dominguez Mrs. Marcia Zorrilla, Ms. Natalee Ernstrom, Ms. Selma Schlesinger, Ms. Susan Obata, Mr. Victor Travis, Ms. Sylvia Lewis, and Mrs. Carisa Veridiano, thank you for allowing me to enhance my counseling skills with your staff. In the short time I have known all of you, my counseling skills have grown immensely. I attribute that to the caring and nurturing environment that you provide on a daily basis to the staff and students of Balboa High School.

To my colleague Mr. Marcus Armstrong, you already know how much I respect you. I appreciate your passion for law. Especially, your zeal, desire and tenacity for practicing law. I look forward to seeing you stand before a judge and court system one day as a profoundly enthusiastic polished attorney.

To all of my strong Black male and female colleagues at Sankofa, I send you a powerful greeting from our Yoruba ancestry – Ase! I would also like to thank all of you including, Mr. and Mrs. Claudius and Jenee Johnson, Mr. Eric Taylor, Mr. Tyrone Cannon, Ms. Alexis Cobbins, Ms. Brianna Moore and Mr. Kenny Hall. Thank you for allowing me this opportunity to utilize my Afrocentric gift of counseling with the Black families across the greater San Francisco Bay Area.

Thank you Mr. and Mrs. Claudius and Jenee Johnson for mentoring to me the true spirit of the Black Family. Claudius, as I stated in an earlier acknowledgement, words cannot describe how much you blessed me in my life! In the short time I have known you, you helped me redefine my Blackness – giving me self-confidence, Black Pride and boosting my will and desire to do anything I want to do in this entire world! May God continue to bless you and your entire family for taking over where many of our Black men have failed to do – show up consistently!

I would like to acknowledge and thank all of my colleagues at the Children's Council! Thank you Dr. Farris Page, Maiysha Dickerson, Jessica Boehme, Gena Lindsay, Bonnie Liang, Mae Feng, Ruth Rodriguez, Susan Erickson, Kelvin Arenas, Michael Williams and Jennifer Chambers. Thank you all for allowing me to develop my mental health consulting skills with your organization.

I give special thanks to Dr. Farris Page for being my mentor in the field of mental health. Your profound knowledge and expertise in early childhood education has been pivotal in renovating the entire Children's Council organization, particularly providing quality mental health training for early childhood care providers in the most impoverished and diverse communities of San Francisco, California.

I would also like to give a special thanks to my clinical supervisor Dr. Charles Brinamen at the Children's Council for your inspirational way of supervising. I am so grateful that I was able to benefit from your wisdom, attentive listening and ever-probing questioning of my therapeutic modality and stance.

To Mrs. Amy Lean Fogliani, thank you for boosting my career with your expertise marketing skills. Your strategic methods of marketing and promotion have increased my professional platform exponentially as a mental health and educational consultant. Most important, thank you for being consistent, genuine, and dependable.

Most significant, I must thank my FedEx Kinkos family members at both the Richmond District and Sloat locations. Thank all of you including, Sabrina, Marcos, Shawn, Stefan, Saidah, Sayed, Jimmy, Mike, John and Kim. You all have been a tremendous blessing because of your helpfulness and technological assistance.

To my UPS family; Amit, Tania, Edgar, Ted and Elon. Thank you for always allowing me to utilize your computer, packing and shipping services to enhance my overall professional and personal development. All of you epitomize the high standard of customer service in your own uniquely gifted way.

To all of my professors, counselors and coaching staff at my Alma matter, City College of San Francisco. Thank you for allowing me to grow as a young college student. All of you, in one way or another, offered me support throughout my years as a junior college student. It will never be forgotten! Go Rams!

To all of my professors, counselors and administrative staff at my Alma matter, San Francisco State University. Thank you for mentoring me as I transitioned into becoming a doctoral candidate and future student. Your direct support and counsel, especially the staff at the Educational Opportunity Program (EOP) had a significant impact on my growth as an undergraduate and graduate student. Thank you for all of the educational services you provided me throughout the many years as a fellow Gator!

Most important, I owe a deep gratitude for my mentor and Auntie Dr. Marilyn Stepney at San Francisco State University. Both she and her daughter Kim Stepney helped my mother to raise me in a time when the extended Black family had a profoundly strong presence in the Black community. Thank you Auntie Marilyn for teaching me how to survive in academia where many young Black males do not exist – either as students or professors! I thank God for your counsel every day!

To all of my other extended family members who helped my mom raise me or who have been a big influence in my life, I sincerely thank you! Some include Auntie Linda Midget, Cousin Kim Kimble, Auntie Robbie Austin & Family, Auntie Marie Marshall, Auntie Maxine Arnold, Cousin Tamar Gillette, Cousin Joanna Gillette, Cousin Rebecca Gillette, Cousin Jonathan Gillette, Cousin Abraham Gillette, Auntie Jean Peck and family, Uncle Rosco Westbrook and Auntie Connie, Uncle Flash and Auntie Tammie, Uncle and Auntie Loyal Moore, Cousin Sabrina Reynolds, Cousin Clarissa Ringer, and Uncle Billie and Auntie Mikelyn Threadgill.

Thank you Walee and John at Faxon Garage for always taking care of my truck. Over the past ten years you have been true to your word and have always tried your best to keep my truck running. I sincerely appreciate your expertise and counsel cornering effective vehicle maintenance. Thank you for treating your customers with the utmost respect and care!

In particular, John, I would really like to thank you from the bottom of my heart. I have known you for over twenty years and throughout our friendship you have never lied to me about the condition, maintenance and future of the vehicles I left in your care. Your mechanical expertise has allowed me to have a new inspiration and knowledge for automobiles that I have used strategically over the years. Thank you for being one of the few honest automotive mechanics!

To my fellow Airborne Rangers at the 1/75th Ranger Regiment in Savannah, Georgia and to my 173rd Airborne Paratroopers in Vicenza, Italy I say a heartfelt thank you! I will never forget the training I experienced with both of these elite Army Infantry forces. Being trained at both duty stations allowed me to become the strong Black resilient male that I am today. God Bless you for your valiant service to our country!

And last but not certainly not least thank you to Mr. Will Baab for completing the final book cover presentation. Your ability to complete such a complicated project at the last minute speaks to your expertise and skills as a graphic media designer. I am greatly appreciative for your dedication to this project.

And finally, to anyone who I may have forgotten, thank you for all of your support and encouragement.

DEBORAH GEROSA

"Colours and Shapes of my Heart Art Collection"

My name is Deborah Gerosa. I am truly honored to have been commissioned to paint the cover of this book. I am a local artist who still considers herself a student of art. I feel I will always be learning more, and more each day about the art of painting. "Colours and Shapes of my Heart Art Collection" is what I call my work. The title of the cover painting is: "Birthing Generations."

I am a local girl; born, and raised in San Francisco, California. I am married, and have two sons. I started my journey down the road of visual art (painting) in 1998. Prior to this date, I had never painted anything but the walls in my home. I always say painting discovered me; instead of the other way around. My cousin Edy saw some drawings I had done. She asked me if I could do a drawing for her bathroom. I said, "Sure, I'll give a shot." She then said it would be nice if I could do the piece in watercolor. I then replied, "I don't paint." Well, shortly after that conversation I saw the famous artist "Bob Ross" on his TV show "The Joy of Painting". He was ever so graceful and calm when giving instruction on how to paint with oils. He made it look so easy, the desire to go out, and buy art supplies became overwhelming.

I couldn't ignore the pull. I started painting, and haven't stopped. My subject matters usually involve my own life experiences, and things I admire. I say, my cousin Edy put the idea in my mind, and I begin to wonder if maybe I could paint after all. Watching Bob Ross paint, inspired me to put my wonderment into action. He made it look so simple, so joyful, so peaceful.

The fear of trying was no more. All I begin to feel was that, I needed to hurry up, and get started.

I believe God lined everything up; and continues to inspire me. Painting has truly been a new found love, and joy for me. It would have been nice to have discovered this passion earlier in my life. However, I know God set everything up, and prepared me for this journey to happen just at the right time. I believe when God gives us a gift, it explodes in us in His perfect time - at the time when we can be the most affective. I thank the Lord and Dr. Aaron Horn for the opportunity.

For those interested in Deborah Gerosa's work, please visit http://www.dgsartexperience.com for more information.

AARON L. HORN

Dr. Aaron L. Horn was born and raised as a young child in San Francisco's Bayview-Hunters Point neighborhood. Although he moved away from Bayview as a young child, he has claimed Bayview because of his family of origin and love for his community. Dr. Horn began his career as an educator in the 1990's as a Program Coordinator for a non-profit agency called San Francisco Educational Services, previously located in the Bayview. As a young educator, he enjoyed establishing relationships with students and teachers from various cultures. While working in the community of Bayview, Dr. Horn attended San Francisco State University and completed his Bachelors in Sociology and Masters in Education. It was at this point in Dr.

Horn's career where he began his life-long passion for counseling underserved families.

After finishing his Master's degree, Dr. Horn obtained his teaching credential in History at San Francisco State University. Throughout his academic career, Dr. Horn taught, counseled, and mentored K-12 students in West Contra Costa Unified and San Francisco Unified School District. In 2008, Dr. Horn received his doctorate degree in International Multicultural Education from the University of San Francisco. His research involved investigating the impact of caring relationships on young African American males' education.

After working with underserved families as an educator, Dr. Horn realized that his teaching was becoming more therapeutic. By this means, the families that Dr. Horn was working with began to engage in candid discussions regarding their mental health issues. As a result of these discussions, Dr. Horn decided to re-enroll at the University of San Francisco and pursue his life-long passion of becoming a therapist. In summer 2012, Dr. Horn received his Master's Degree in Counseling Psychology.

For over twenty years, Dr. Horn has devoted his passion to the enhancement of the Bayview-Hunters Point community. He has received numerous awards and accolades, including "Community Advocate Award" from San Francisco State University. Dr. Horn is currently an educational consultant for a non-profit agency called Brainstorm Tutoring, a Mental Health Consultant for the Children's Council and the owner of Horn Development Consulting. All organizations are located in San Francisco, California.

For those interested in Dr. Horn's profession, please visit
http://aaronlhorn.com for more information.

Made in the USA
San Bernardino, CA
26 November 2013